"DADDY" Who Me?

BY

D. Maurice Johnson

© 2002 by D. Maurice Johnson. All rights reserved.

ISBN: 0-7596-9061-8

This book is printed on acid free paper.

ACKNOWLEDGEMENTS

*"Blessed be the Lord God, ...
who only does wondrous things."*
Psalm 72:18

I thank my God Almighty for giving me the opportunity to be a part of the lives of every person mentioned in this book. It has been both my blessing and my Honor.

*****

I offer my heartfelt appreciation to each of these young people, their parents and grandparents; especially the Browers (Al and Nee Nee) and the Agees (Daniel Sr. and Rená). Thank you for sharing your children and lives with me and for granting me permission to share our stories in this book. Much Love to you all!

*****

I lovingly dedicate this book to my cherished brother, Keith, who has always wondered how I could claim other people as my own family, especially my Godchildren. He acknowledges how important these individuals are to me and freely offers himself to them. Thanks, "Mother-Brother," for your loving support and wisdom.

*****

Also, dedicated to my mother, the late Vivian "Sweet" Johnson-Bell, who showered me with her unconditional love and support, and taught me how to share with others by her own example. Even though we practiced different faiths, we both acknowledged that her Allah and my God was (and is) worthy of our constant praise.

iii

PART ONE

D. Maurice Johnson

One

I was about to celebrate my forty "something-th" birthday on Monday.

The Wednesday before my birthday Iisha asked me,

"Dad can we celebrate your birthday on Sunday?

I told her yes.

"What do you want to do?" "What do you want for a present?"

I told her that I wanted to go to Philip's Seafood Restaurant and a bottle of cologne. Phillip's, Red Lobster, and Applebees were some of our favorite hangouts.

She said, "Alright, I'm going to church with you on Sunday and we'll go to the Phillip's in Baltimore, rather than the one in D.C. Iisha was trying to make it easier on me because she knew nothing would happen until I finished my work at the church in Baltimore.

Early Sunday morning there was one message on my answering machine that had been left late Saturday night. I wondered who had called me so late because everyone knows that I go to bed early on Saturday nights. I need to be well rested because Sundays are my primary workday and typically busy days. I pushed the play button on the answering machine and it was Monique calling from Chicago.

"Hey Dad, I know that you're probably in bed, but I wanted to make sure that I did not miss your birthday. I know you have a busy day tomorrow and I will be out most of the day too. Have a wonderful day, Fatha. I love you."

Sunday night I was stretched out on the couch trying to recuperate from Sunday service and Iisha when the phone rang. "Daddy?"

I said, "Yes?"

3

It was Leroy calling from Indianapolis.

"Me and Simone are calling to wish you a happy birthday in advance. We figured you would be out celebrating on Monday and we did not want to miss you."

He and I chatted about other things for another 15 minutes.

Shortly after hanging up with Leroy, the phone rang again. I was thinking to myself, "This phone is ringing off the hook! AND it's giving me gas!"

"Pop?" I said, "Yes, Sir?"

I was just calling to wish you a happy birthday, old man."

I said, "Thank you, Sir."

It was Charles calling from Tennessee. We also talked for a while. Then I resumed my position on the couch watching TV for a while before I finally went to bed. The phone did not ring anymore that night.

On Monday mornings I usually check my email messages. I got one particular message that read:

"Hey, happy birthday, I wish I could have been there to celebrate with you."

It was Yeolman emailing me from South Carolina.

The day after my birthday, I got a belated birthday call.

"Happy belated Birthday, Champ. What's up with ya?"

It was Willie calling. He lives in Maryland area as well.

"I'm sorry that I didn't remember to call you on your birthday. I wish I could have been there to hang out with you, but so many things were going on."

I said, "That's OK, son. Thanks for calling to wish me a happy birthday. I know you would have been here if you could."

Later on that week, I was warmly ruminating over the many birthday expressions that I had received, when it suddenly dawned on me that I had not gotten a call from Little DJ and

Dre, nor had I gotten a call from AJ and Brianna. I have gotten so used to hearing their sweet little innocent and angelic voices singing, "Happy Birthday, Dear DJ. Happy Birthday to you."

I also found myself really wishing that I could have gotten birthday calls from Christina and David and a few others.

When I finally did see Brianna and AJ at church, her father told me she had something for me. She came running up to me looking just like a little "doll baby" princess with a really big grin on her face. Her beautiful brown eyes were beaming up at me. She excitedly handed me a clear zip lock sandwich bag that was filled with goodies. It contained a muffin, several pieces of candy and some bubble gum.

She said, "Happy birthday, DJ!"

While I was thanking her with hugs and kisses, AJ walked up with his hands stuffed in his pockets and a sheepish grin on his face that suggested, "I'm waiting for my hugs and kisses too." He said, "Happy birthday, DJ!"

So I immediately repeated the process. I thanked him with hugs and kisses as well. What else was I supposed to do?

Two

My father, Sterling Jr. is the son of Anderson and Hazel (Cross) Johnson. He was born in the steel mill town of East Chicago, Indiana and raised in the section called Indiana Harbor or "the Harbor." His father raised him in a single parent home. I'm told they called his father, "Papa." He died before I was born so I never had a chance to meet him. My father did not meet his mother until he was sixteen years old. "Papa" had only provided dad with food and shelter. Everything else was left up to him. Dad did say that he received additional support and nurture from a variety of women in the community and females who were friends of his father. My father only had a few males that he considered his close friends. Daddy worked at Inland Steel and consistently engaged in several other business ventures on the side to generate additional revenue. In later years he told me he did that to provide for his children.

Many of my memories about what happened during that period are sketchy. It was not until I was about twenty-five that I learned most of what I now know about my father. What I learned came from him, my mother, maternal grandmother, and brother, Keith.

There are several memories of my dad that I never shall forget. One was when my father had gotten sick after he and my mother had divorced. I went into my mother's bedroom and found him in her bed sleeping! Another time, he was hungry, so, he was allowed to have dinner with us. Then there was the time, when my mother got sick. He came to visit us every day, especially while she was convalescing. I always seemed to be comforted when he was allowed to do things with us that included my mother. For example, He would take us to worship at the Islamic Mosque, the "temple," or help us carry large bags of clothes to the laundry. Dad would carry us on his shoulders while we walked places, or he would drive us places when he finally got a car. Also, he knew that I could not bear being cold. When I would be shivering from the cold, he would carry me to the bathroom, which was the hottest room in the entire apartment. Once, Dad mailed me a pair of pilot's wings from American Airlines because he knew how badly I wanted to learn how to fly. One Saturday evening I was alone in the church practicing on the organ and I thought I was alone, but he was standing there listening to me with a great big smile on his face.

Overall, the childhood memory of my dad that is most poignant in my mind is, even though he did not physically reside with us, we would see him regularly enough to know who he was. Some of dad's visits were expected and others were unexpected. But, we all knew he would definitely show up for our high school graduations! Most of the time, he showed up unexpectedly. I believe he did that on purpose to keep us on our toes behaviorally and also to remind us that he was still there for us. Dad would always bring something for us. I can recall the time when he showed up and we excitedly ran to his Chevy. We found a great big bag of goodies just for us. There were things like underclothes, socks, shirts, sweaters, belts and ties. Another time, while we we're playing in the yard, an eighteen-wheel truck pulled up in front of our house. Dad had bicycles shipped to us. He had truly made us happy that day!

My father and mother, "Sweet" divorced when I was about six years old. I must commend both my parents, because neither of them ever said anything negative about the other to me. I do not recall ever witnessing them having arguments, even though I'm sure they occurred. However, my parents did leave me with one very powerful adult memory. They had grown to the point where they could be friends with each other. When I graduated from Southern Methodist University (SMU), they both were present. They were headed toward the gymnasium where my commencement was being held. Dad was supporting "Sweet" who was having shortness of breath because of her heart condition. But "Sweet" was also supporting him as he walked slightly bent forward due to the usual aches and pains in his legs. He refers to them as the aches and pains of getting older. It really made my heart glad to watch both my parents leisurely strolling across the campus arm-in-arm.

Dad remarried twice and produced children from both of those unions. He always shared that aspect of his life with us. We visited him at his home and spent time with our stepsisters. In fact, it was his last wife, Catherine or "Kitty" who invited me to move to Washington, D.C. to live with them when I was 25 years old. The move was a big adjustment for me. I moved to D.C. unconsciously expecting to be treated like my father's child-son, even though I had been living as an independent adult in Indiana since I was seventeen years old. The move was really good for me, because I had fallen into a terrible rut that was keeping me from growing. They were quite encouraging to me while I was seeking employment and simultaneously matriculating through Howard University. I doubt very seriously that I would have ever graduated from college without their support.

During graduate school, I sought professional counseling to deal with my anger issues. It was one of the best things that ever happened to me because I got a chance to look candidly at myself and to begin to make sense of all the experiences that have helped shape me. As I better began to understand myself, I discovered that most of my beliefs, values, emotional responses, and habits were linked to my desire to have a deeper, more meaningful relationship with my own father. I also began to really understand things from my father's perspective and to empathize with his past decisions. I was able to see my father with new eyes when I returned to D.C.! I was now able to celebrate his life (and his presence in my life) and he was able to reciprocate. I recall telling him something about myself that I did not think would be very pleasant for him to hear. His face showed no emotion as he listened silently and nodded his head. He simply replied, "OK," and left the room. Shortly after our conversation, I went visiting at a friend's house. The whole time there I wondered how Dad was responding to our conversation. When I returned home, there was a note from him on my bed:

> *"You are my son and I love you. Nothing you do will ever change that!*
>
> *"Love, Daddy"*

From that day on, we worked very hard at establishing a closer relationship. We have had times of mutual sharing, exploring, misunderstanding, frustrations, confrontations, challenges, and painful confessions. Those were some very trying and scary times, but we kept working at it until we had eventually worked through them. On the other hand, we have also shared many times of celebration, joy, laughter, and fun. (Usually when I was trying to sleep!) My Dad could be such a clown, especially when my friends came to visit. They enjoyed "Papa Joe" as much as I did! We nicknamed him "Papa Joe" because he looked so content the many times we found him holding my infant nephew asleep on his gut while he watched TV. From the aforementioned experiences, we have bonded and developed a level of intimacy that I will never be able to articulate. Not only, did we enjoy a close profound father-son relationship; we were confidants and sounding boards for each other.

During this same time period, Dad and Kitty made me aware of a Minister of Music position at Gethsemane Baptist Church. I was not interested in that position or a position in any other church! I had grown so tired of church politics, the exploitation and domination of insecure pastors, and haggling for a decent [live-able] salary with those cheap official boards! I had made a personal vow not to play for any more churches. For weeks the both of them persisted that I at least interview. So, I did – reluctantly - just so they would leave me alone. Well, my tenure there lasted nearly four years. [Thank you, Dad and Kitty.]

I was so happy the first time Dad attended one of the services. It dawned on me one day that he was attending on a regular basis. He often came home from church telling everyone he was "proud of me and the work I was doing." What he failed to say was that **DURING EVERY VISIT**, he cried the whole time he was there. (Actually, several people mentioned this.) Also, while there, I was ordained as a Minister of the Gospel. When my father joined the church a year later, I had the distinct honor of baptizing him. I initiated and welcomed my Dad into the body of Christ! This was significant to me because he had chosen to forsake his Islamic beliefs. In other words, we now share the same Faith – the Christian Faith! Another thing that happened was my father, who was not a singer, sang with a special Men's choir in observance of our Annual Men's Day celebration. My Dad said he was nervous, but it was fun. That was one way I challenged my father.

There was another challenge for Dad that I helped to facilitate. Our family did not know much about our paternal or maternal lineages. Keith and I worried Dad about our ancestors on his side of the family so much that he got tired. Shortly afterward, Dad told me that he had been given a spiritual mission to find out more about his family. That search led him to his mother's birthplace, Clarksville, Tennessee around 1993. It was there that he began (and continues) the quest for his relatives. First, he found his paternal side, the Webb-Frost relatives from Eufaula, Alabama. Then, he found his maternal side, the Joiner-Cross relatives in Clarksville and Hopkinsville, Tennessee.

His search has been quite extensive. He has talked with so many people who are friends, neighbors, and newly found relatives. He has spent many hours, days, months and years doing research. Some of the sources that have been helpful to him are the newspapers and the historic archives. He found several hundred birth and death certificates, marriage and divorce licenses, death notices, and cemetery plots. His concern for poor condition of those cemeteries, attracted so much media attention that they are now in better condition (thanks to him) and listed in the National Cemetery Registry. He loves to tell us the stories about him cleaning graves and finding the graves of our unknown relatives. He is always amazed that he goes in search of one thing, but finds something else. He says, "God is so amazing. He continues to let me know that I don't control anything and that he will show me what he wants me to know in his own time." He has inundated us with clippings, articles, and photos of the things he has discovered. When I asked what he wants us to do with all the discoveries, he initially responded, "nothing." As I probed deeper, he responded, "Pass it." Finally, after much probing, his real desire is that Keith and I publish it as a book.

After my marriage fell apart, I was disappointed that Dad had not shared the "ins-and-outs" and "do's and don'ts" of marriage with me. When I approached him, he acknowledged his failure to get involved. His response was that it was not his place and experience was the best teacher. Dad had not considered that I had no role model of what to expect, or what to do in marriage even before things began to deteriorate. He only understood what I meant after I explained to him that I needed him and depended upon his wisdom from experiencing the similar predicaments on more than one occasion. After that, we were able to have a long, candid discussion about his view of women, his expectations in marriage, the problems that he encountered, and how he dealt with them. What I quickly discovered is that we were very similar in each of those aspects. We both vowed not to do things like our father's had, but, when it was all over, we had done exactly what we had vowed not to do.

The last thing I wish to share is Dad's efforts within the last few years. Dad attended his first Frost family reunion in Eufaula, Alabama in 1997. Dad, Keith and my family attended the Frost family reunion in Houston, Texas in 1998. Dad hosted the first Johnson Family Retreat for my siblings in Clarksville in 1999. I was initially reluctant and apprehensive since it was the first time all of us had gathered together after my mother's death in 1995. It was really tense amongst us during that time until Dad stepped in to stabilize us. Since that time communication has been very nil or very strained – if it existed at all. Despite my concerns, dad still proceeded with the retreat. To my surprise, it was a good thing that I attended. I was surprised that we could move from the painful past into the precocious present and look forward to future positive relationships. It was refreshing to experience the playful interaction and bonding of my nieces and nephews. It was even more important that my siblings and I reconnected with each other. Dad made all of that possible and it felt really good. My sister in Cincinnati, Ohio hosted the second Family Retreat on Memorial Day 2000.

Dad considers three events significant to his growth process and healing. First, the pride he felt when he attended my Senior Recital at Howard University. Second, his determination to visit me in Dallas even though that would "burn Kitty up." Third, when I was hospitalized in 1992, he sensed that I knew he would come and that I expected he would appear. I am not sure what meaning he has assigned to these events, because he did not say. My guess is that he was reinforcing the basic premise of this book, which is the importance and influence of the presence of a father figure.

One of the best things that have ever happened in my entire life was restoring my relationship with my father, my Papa. Being reconnected with my father helped me to heal. I began to make sense of my life, and I grew up. I felt like I belonged. I cherish our relationship and thank God for giving us to each other.

Three

"Mr. Bob" lived next-door to us on Pulaski Street in "the Harbor." I met him during the snowstorm of 1967. He asked me to shovel the snow in his yard. When I finished he paid me a whole five dollars! That was the beginning of a relationship that was very special.

Mr. Bob was in his early fifties. He was a very soft-spoken, low-key man who kept to himself. I'm not sure whether he was a recluse or an introvert. There was only a few times that I ever saw him with anyone. Those times were purely by accident when I happened to bump into him on the street. He was a bachelor with no children. He never spoke of his family until about ten years later, which were the latter years of his life. By then our relationship had weathered several significant shifts and matured.

Little did I know that Mr. Bob knew, and had known, my family very well for many years. In fact, he lived in the very same apartment that my paternal grandfather, "Papa" had lived. Mr. Bob's told me a few stories that helped me know the kind of man "Papa" was.

Mr. Bob also knew that my parents were divorced and that my mother was struggling to raise us alone dependent upon the welfare system and child support. He knew that she and my eight siblings were living in the rear ground floor apartment of a building that contained four apartments. Our apartment had a living room, kitchen, split bathrooms: one long room with the toilet and another tiny room under the stairs with a bathtub, and two small bedrooms. He saw us carry large trash bags of clothes to the laundry (if there was money for it) and later told me that he had often wondered if we had enough food to eat.

Needless to say, I always looked forward to seeing Mr. Bob! He would always give me pocket money and feed me.

A shift took place when I began to realize every time I saw him he would do the exact same thing. I began to wait around hoping to see him. When he noticed that I had begun to wait around for him, he told me that he did not have a phone and that he worked a lot at different hours of the day. He worked at the local pool hall (the Poolroom) as a crap table operator. In order to stop me from hanging around waiting for him he provided me with two options. I could call the Poolroom and leave a message or I could send one of the guys inside to find him. But he strictly and emphatically forbade me to come into the poolroom at any time!

Another shift occurred several years later when I found the courage to ask him for money to buy things that I wanted. I almost "chickened out!" I was so ashamed for having to ask and very scared that he would say no. I was afraid that he would think I was only being around him to get money. I hoped that he would not abandon me. Fortunately, he graciously gave me what I asked and told me, "Don't worry, just find me and ask me for whatever you need." I was so relieved and excited.

The next shift occurred when we began to spend personal time together. The first time, we went to a local Men's store for my first tailor made suit and to a local bookstore where he insisted that I buy a book. Then, the trips moved beyond East Chicago to stores in other nearby cities like Goldblatts in Hammond or Sears in Gary. The ultimate trip for me was when we took the South Shore train to "the Loop" or downtown Chicago. Every trip followed the same format: shop for clothes, eat, and buy a book (or books). He would always tell me, "You spend more money for good clothes but they last longer. You look and feel better when you wear nice clothes." Then he would say, "Ok, now let's go get a book. You can't wear nice clothes and have an empty head. You avoid that by reading."

After several years, I began to call Mr. Bob my godfather. He never told me that I could not refer to him as that, nor did he ever refer to me as his godson, that I know of. But his actions and attitude showed me that he was OK with the fact that I chose him to fill that role in my life. On his birthday and Father's day I always gave him cards, which said "from your godson." Both of my parents were OK with him being my godfather and graciously shared me with him. They respected my choice and him, and they appreciated his willingness to share with me.

Mr. Bob was very excited when I began to grow into a young adult. I had completed High School and was playing the piano at Zion Baptist Church. In fact, I was playing for several other churches and attending Computer Programming School. Although he never attended church or heard me play music, he repeatedly told me that he was proud of me, and the things that I was doing. That felt really good. On occasion he would still buy me clothes and educational books (sometimes he would even let me get fun books). My physical interaction with Mr. Bob was not quite as frequent after I got my first apartment in Hammond. I supported myself by simultaneously working as Minister of Music and a computer operator for Lake County. I had also enrolled in studies at Purdue University in Hammond. We did manage to maintain some communication by telephone.

After being on my own for several years, there was a period that I was not able to contact Mr. Bob for several weeks. I now was working as a computer operator at a Bank in Chicago and he had moved on Catalpa Street. There was no answer at his new number during the hours that I knew he was usually home. I really got worried when no one at the Poolroom had seen him.

Then one day I got a call from one of his nieces who lived in Chicago. They had found my phone number in Mr. Bob's apartment and called to tell me that he was in St. Catherine's Hospital with severe pneumonia.

My heart was broken when I saw Mr. Bob lying in that hospital bed with tubes everywhere and oxygen tubes in his nostrils. His breathing was laborious and he was constantly coughing up large amounts of dark green slime. When he saw me his eyes lit up. He tried to talk to me but the thick green slime made it very difficult. He extended a trembling hand out to grab mine and squeezed it. With tears in my eyes, I bent over, hugged him and kissed his forehead. He calmed down and settled into a semi-comfortable resting state. It hurt me so bad to see Mr. Bob like that. He seemed so weak, helpless, and miserable.

I met Mr. Bob's only surviving family members. He had told me that they existed, but never mentioned them by name or spoke of them in any great length. His two nieces from Chicago, Illinois were both women in their fifties with children and grandchildren. They immediately accepted me as their extended family, because I was "Uncle Robert's" godson. We embraced and exchanged telephone numbers. For several days, all I had time to do was go to work 50 miles away and spend 3-4 hours in East Chicago sitting with and caring for Mr. Bob at the hospital. Just when I was getting settled into this routine, the hospital called me at work to inform that Mr. Bob had taken a turn for the worse. By the time, I arrived Mr. Bob was dead. I said my goodbye, and with tears in my eyes, I bent over, hugged him and kissed his forehead.

Helping the family make his funeral arrangements was very painful and emotionally draining. I had never experienced the death of a person that was close to me, because all of my immediate family members were still alive. Fortunately, I found a source of comfort and strength from my faith in God and the loving support of his two nieces and their families. They even listed me in his Obituary as part of the family. What an honor Mr. Bob and his family had bestowed upon me!

I truly miss Mr. Bob. His legacy is very much alive in me. It is reflected in my taste in fine quality clothing (and willingness to invest in them) and the pleasure I receive from being an avid reader without regard for the subject matter. My interest in reading stimulated me to achieve my own personal goal of matriculation through the entire educational system, establish an extensive and varied personal library, and to author (and publish) books in several disciplines. I believe I have subconsciously acquired (and prefer) his personal style as a recluse and introvert.

Most of all, I inherited from him a servant's heart. He reached out to an impoverished teenager. He showed me love, care, support, and appreciation for the finer things in life. He also challenged me to know more, become more, and to be the best at whatever I desired. He showed me that all things are within my grasp, but I must reach for it and take care of what I attain. Those who know me will be able to see how similar my character is to Mr. Bob's. He demonstrated the powerful and long-lasting effect that a positive male figure can make in a child's life and development. It has been my honor to have known such a classy gentleman as Mr. Bob. May his soul rest in God's peace, forever.

Four

In 1969, I wanted to join Zion Baptist Church. But my parents continued to confess their Islamic faith and practice Muslim beliefs. I was disappointed when my mother told me I was too young to make that decision at the time. However, I continued to visit on occasion because many of my classmates at Washington High School attended Zion. My Elementary School music teacher was the Minister of Music and all of the friends I hung out with (and their families) either sang in one of the choirs or were involved in one of the ministries at Zion.

Oh how I loved to watch the processional as the choir jubilantly sang, "It's a Highway to Heaven." They boldly marched down all three long aisles, up the stairs (6-9 feet) to a high middle choir loft and the two smaller choir lofts on each side of the pulpit (3-3 feet). I had so many dreams of that grand processional that I became inspired to play music in Church. At home I would pretend I was playing the piano on any flat surface that I could find, i.e., tabletops or the stairs or even windowsills. The vision of the choir processional haunted me for quite some time. Two years later, I joined Zion on Tuesday night of a revival without my parent's consent. I was so afraid they would not understand and forbid me to accept the Christian faith. Much to my surprise they honored my decision, even though I was just 14 years old! That was the beginning of my relationship with "Reverend."

When I became a member, "Reverend" had already been the pastor for several years. He was a young pastor in his mid-thirties. He could really preach and teach the good news, plus he could sing! He was a strong advocate for Christian Education. In fact, he insisted that every member of the church attend Sunday school. "Reverend" was an excellent Pastor: a

19

warm man with a kind heart who loved people, especially young people. If he missed you at church on Sunday, he would personally call to check on you. He visited the sick in the hospital and at their homes. He would leave revivals or conventions early to come home and bury members or comfort their families. He would help people find jobs and get out of financial hardships. He was quick to share his resources with those who needed them, even if they were not members of Zion. I can still remember how he was always able to touch the coldest and meanest members with his charm. He knew his members! He spent long hours in the office as an administrator. He was a visionary, plus he was organized, thorough and diligent.

"Reverend" was married and had a brand new baby son. Over the years his family increased to include two daughters. His wife was a musician and each of his children were involved in music training. They played for Zion when they grew older. He was the oldest son of the pastor of a Church in Nebraska. He had four other siblings: an older sister, a brother who was also a preacher and two sisters who were musicians. They had a close-knit family so you could imagine how much "Reverend" stressed family unity at Zion. Every year Zion would journey to different states to fellowship with other churches. On alternating years we would make pilgrimages to Omaha. Even though he was our pastor, "Reverend" was a nationally known and well-respected Evangelist. He conducted lots of revivals and was heavily involved in the city, district, state and national conventions. Hence, we were always traveling and seeing new ways to do things as a Church.

Zion and "Reverend" became a major social outlet for us teenagers. We were always around him at Choir rehearsals, Sunday school, Bible study and prayer meetings, and even the church meetings. He always seemed to make time for fellowship with us whether it was just hanging around the church or at a restaurant or at his home. We would even travel for hours to surprise him at his out of town preaching engagements. Because we were close to him, we also experienced his playful nature and jokes.

I got close to "Reverend" and his family because of my interest in playing music and their love for music. I could not afford piano lessons, (we were barely surviving) so my maternal grandmother offered to pay for me to take lessons. The drawback was that I needed a piano to practice, which we could not afford either. Piano rentals were unheard of in those days. Even if we could afford to rent a piano where would we have put it? Our cramped two-bedroom apartment barely held our family or our clothes!

"Reverend" allowed me unlimited access to the church's organ and piano, which were kept locked when not in use. The keys to the instruments were kept on a nail in the kitchen of the parsonage, which was adjacent to the Church. Most of the time I gained access to the church and the keys by going through his house. During my senior year of high school I attended classes on a half-day schedule, so I spent most afternoons [and evenings] either in the practice room adjacent to the band room or walked three blocks to Zion. A typical day of practice was a minimum of seven hours, seven days per week! I would practice every time I got near a piano.

After several months, I had gained enough courage to play in public. My skills and knowledge were increasing but my musician friends and some members of Zion did not think so. They complained about my loud volume level, poor sense of timing and lack of experience. When "Reverend" heard about the way I was being treated, he was furious. During the next worship service, he told the congregation to leave me alone because I was learning how to play and that I was going to practice on them. He admonished them to encourage me rather than discourage me.

From that point on, I spent countless hours, at all times of the day and night, playing the organ and the piano in private and public. I would play before, during and after, choir rehearsals, Sunday school and BTU (Baptist Training Union), Worship services, Bible study and prayer meetings, and business meetings. Because of what "Reverend" had said, all the musicians and a few older women choir members would sit with me while I learned to play hymns and other songs they sang. They would say, "The song goes like this, Baby. Do you have it?" They patiently sang over and over to me while I found the chords and established tempos. Once they were able to recognize and keep up with what I was playing they would say, "Yeah, That's it, Baby. You got it!" I knew I had arrived the first time I played for a service all by myself. It was a funeral! I was scared to death. Probably even more so because I was on my own, than because of the eerie nature of the service and the presence of a corpse at the other end of the piano.

My confidence level quickly increased after that experience. My opportunities to perform and travel increased drastically. I began to accompany "Reverend" when he preached at local churches, out of town revivals, the National Sunday School and BTU Congresses, as well as the regional, state and national conventions. I traveled with "Reverend" so much that people began to think I was his biological son. He and his wife treated me as if I was their son. I don't think I ever called him my godfather or dad, but I did give him cards on holidays that referred to him in those terms. I just treated him as if he was my parent and he accepted it. He used to make sure that I was presentable for services. He tied my ties and taught me to how to tie my own tie. He even taught me how to drive on the highway, which I enjoyed because that meant I got to practice driving his white 98 Oldsmobile.

"Reverend" began to encourage me to branch out to play at other churches besides Zion. At age 16, I accepted my first position as musician for the Youth Choir at Friendship Baptist Church in East Chicago once per month. Simultaneously, I volunteered to be one of the musicians for the Northern Indiana Voices of Deliverance Community Choir founded by the late, Gregory Clark. "Northern," was comprised of youth, i.e., musicians and singers from various churches in the Tri-city area: East Chicago, Gary and Hammond, Indiana. Greg later became my peer, my roommate, and a musician at Zion. He really helped me with the rhythmic problems and improvisation skills. Those experiences allowed me to improve my musical skills, own my identity as a musician, and gain access to the wider network of church musicians.

At age 17 another shift occurred. I was elected as Organist for the Youth Division of the State Missionary Baptist Convention and began to attend the annual sessions of the Gospel Music Workshop of America. I reluctantly agreed (because "Reverend" asked) to go play for a pastor friend of his once per month. I accepted the position as musician for the Youth Choir of Tarrytown Baptist Church in Gary. I was surprised by my work there! Within nine months the pastor had asked me to become Minister of Music. I really struggled. I did not want to give up Zion or Friendship, but "Reverend" insisted that I make a choice and stick to it. Needless to say, I accepted the position.

The impact that "Reverend" had on me has been multifaceted. He encouraged me and protected me. He gave me the opportunity to cultivate a solid work ethic by coordinating the Bus Ministry and doing light receptionist work in the office, which exposed me to church administration (and politics). I remember typing his sermons and him reminding me to be accurate, by saying, "words are my business." He showed me how to be a Christian and a professional, to take pride in my musical gift and my public appearance (dress) from the perspective of a leader. He encouraged caring, sharing, education, growth and development.

"Reverend" instilled in me a servant's heart and a passion for ministry with people of all ages. His influence thoroughly equipped me for a career ministry as a career vocation. Due to the many things I have experienced with him, I became a capable student-leader at Tarrytown. Being at Tarrytown allowed me to explore and further refine my knowledge and skills about church and music administration, relationships with pastors and official boards, finances, organization, staff supervision and development, program planning and evaluation, personal and interpersonal communication (oral and written), and techniques for conflict management and resolution.

After reading about "Reverend," those who have experienced me will quickly see his personality. We are similar in that we share a professional demeanor, a sense of integrity and confident leadership, the administrative and organizational skills, a willingness to travel to perform ministry and attend conventions, a strong sense of the care and concern for people, a witty sense of humor, an emphasis on educational growth, a flair for clothes and shoes. "Reverend" showed me how to care. Through him I have met so many people who have shown me how to love and care because they modeled it for me.

Five

"Mr. Jones," is an older gentleman, probably around Mr. Bob's age. I met him at Zion after being a member there for several years. He is a native of Shreveport, Louisiana, but became a resident of Indiana for many years after a tour of duty in the military. His immediate family consists of a wife, a daughter, and a granddaughter. All the members of Mrs. Jones' family also attended Zion. They already knew me because I was a musician at Zion, but I really didn't know who they were until I found out that one of my closest peers in High School was part of Mr. Jones' family by marriage. "Mr. Jones" mentioned having brothers and sisters, but I'm not sure how many or their names or where they lived exactly.

By Profession "Mr. Jones" was a presser at a dry cleaners. At Zion, he worked on the finance committee. He and his team would be counting the offerings long after church had ended. I used to be one of the last people to leave the church because I was either socializing or practicing. That was the time we saw and got to know each other. One day he offered me a ride home because he was going to make a deposit at the bank near where I lived. On several other occasions he gave me rides. Our rides became more and more regular. I enjoyed the rides because we talked about church, our families, and how I was progressing in school. He seemed genuinely interested in me. During a very trying period in my life, he told me to let him know if I ever needed anything.

One day "Mr. Jones" said his wife had told him to invite me to their home in Gary for dinner. I was honored and graciously accepted. The time also came when I had to take him up on his offer to help. He graciously helped me and restated his willingness to help. I think we all immediately sensed a unique bond that instinctively graduated into a kinship. I do not remember how it happened, what I do remember is that we began to think of each other not as god-family, but as a family unit! I visited their home regularly, especially on holidays, and was treated like their son. In conversations, he was Daddy, she was Mama, and the daughter was sister. What a great feeling it was to be treated like the only boy in the family.

"Mr. Jones" fulfilled my need to have a special place to belong and allowed me to experience the security of a family unit. It was fun sharing quality family time that included joys and sorrows. I really cherish the many things that I experienced in this great new family relationship. "Mr. Jones" taught me about adulthood from a male perspective, and the basics of using credit to your advantage. He always insisted that I handle my business correctly. I am grateful for the many, many things that he has shown me, especially his caring heart and sharing spirit.

Six

I met "Big Daddy" in 1983 through his wife. I had just moved to Washington, D.C. and accepted a position as Music Director at Greater Mount Zion Baptist Church. Mrs. Knight caught my attention because her salt and pepper colored hair was *always* in place every time I saw her singing alto in the "Sincere Echoes" choir. I thought to myself, "that's a classy lady!" Not only that, she had a very caring nature. As time progressed they invited me to their home and into their life. I learned very quickly that *they* were a classy middle-aged couple!

When I asked the Knights if they would be my godparents, they graciously accepted. I began to call her "Ma" but I was a little uncomfortable calling him anything other than "Knight," which is what everyone else called him. I think it was because I sensed he had not really accepted me as his godson. I made sure to give him cards that referred to him as God Dad, but eventually I just gave him cards for Dads. I was struggling with how to address him as my God Dad. I was so glad when "Ma" referred to him as my "Big Daddy." That was the solution to my dilemma and I have been calling him that ever since!

When I introduced the Knights to my parents and friends they accepted them as my Godparents without reservation or resentment. They were very happy about my relationship with the Knights. Even my maternal grandmother met them and liked them. They would even exchange Christmas cards! The Knights did the same with their family and friends. They got the same responses as I did from my family and friends. Our families, friends and the members of Greater Mount Zion were always inquiring, "How's your Mom and Dad?" Or "How's that son of yours?" In our family times together we would happily report to who inquired and who sent "hello" messages.

The members of "Big Daddy's" family are his daughter, from his previous marriage; her two children, a boy and girl; one brother and a very close niece in Topeka, Kansas. His late mother also lived in Kansas until the time of her death. "Big Daddy" retired from the Air Force and the Department of Education. I found it ironic that we had never met because he lived in East Chicago for many years prior to moving to Washington, D.C. He is quiet observant and typically interacts in a unique low-key and mild manner. Once he becomes comfortable, he speaks from a confident demeanor in a very commanding voice, and exhibits a great sense of humor. We are amazed at his gift for cultivating natural things. He loves to landscape the yard and work in his garden. He gives most of the vegetables away to other people. He is good - so are the things from his garden!

"Big Daddy" loves to tease "Ma" when we get together. We tease him because he loves electronic devices like TVs, VCRs, Stereos, and telephones. He made "Ma" furious every time he bought things on an impulse. She has learned to be careful not to verbalize what she likes but does not really want, because he would go buy it without any notice. "Big Daddy" always buys the best things; usually they were expensive. She chuckles when she says, "Chile, I'll look up and he'll be bringing it through that door! But he's a good man because he means well. He is sensitive and a caring man with a heart of gold." She's right! He has done the same thing with me several times.

I was the son that neither of them ever had. As with the Jones Family, we celebrated holidays, birthdays, anniversaries and daily life. It was fun sharing quality time as a quaint little family of three. Everyone at Greater Mount Zion knew they were my Godparents and acknowledged our special relationship; they saw it firsthand. After I accepted my calling to the ministry, they made sure that I was always dressed nice and neat. While attending graduate school in Dallas, Texas, they called regularly and sent care packages to my dormitory for those three trying years. Since I have returned to the Washington, D.C. area in 1990, they have continued to support me in the ministry and encouraged me while I established myself in an apartment (and later a house) and even as I completed my Doctor of Ministry Degree.

Throughout the years, my relationship with "Big Daddy" has become more and more special. We talk about real life issues, such as death and dying, marriage and divorce, and spousal relationships. He was furious at how spontaneously I announced I was getting married and even more furious when I announced I was getting a divorce. He really let me have it for not consulting him before I entered into either of those life cycle transitions. We also had to cultivate our own unique style of conflict management and resolution, from both the father-son perspective and the adult-adult perspective. It was a challenge, but it also reassured me that our relationship could weather the storms of life over time. We just had to be willing to respect and understand each other, and communicate honestly.

I also had to ask forgiveness for not seeking his wise counsel in advance and for operating in a vacuum. I had not trusted our relationship enough to include him as part of my inner circle. "Big Daddy" responded like a father should have. He held me accountable for my decisions and behavior. I had not shared with him so he could protect me or give me direction. Which I now understand to be his proper role because I choose to be his son and he chose to be my father figure.

From "Big Daddy" I learned how to be attentive to your mate and how to be a good provider. In his own unique way, I saw him be the head of his household but also show the sensitive and caring male side that must accompany that awesome responsibility. His actions showed me things that he would never utter from his lips. He reinforced what I had experienced with all the other father figures, "Be the Best, get the best and take care of it so that it will last."

Seven

My first recollection of meeting D. Maurice Johnson was at the Seminary on the beautiful, spacious, and well-kept grounds of SMU in Dallas. I was dead broke! I was living in a [dormitory] apartment upstairs from his. It just so happened that I was walking down the hallway and ran into him. We just started a casual conversation and somewhere in conversation he said to me,

"Are you hungry, Herb?"

And Lord only knows I was starving and I had nothing to eat!

He said, "Come on in. I don't have a lot, but what I have you're welcome to."

We sat down and we ate. And from that first meal together to this very day, we have shared one with another [just like biological brothers would do]. He helped me to grow and I have helped him to grow.

You see, in D. Maurice Johnson I have found a well-grounded individual. A man who has come from adversity; who has come from [meager economic conditions], who has come from a family that has been less than ideal. He was definitely not one of the privileged children of America. He [is], if anything other than that, been raised with no "spoon" [with] which to drink his soup.

He grew up in Indiana, the son of divorced parents. His family often had no money and only a handful of people around the community who looked out for him. One of them being the pastor of a church that allowed him to come in after school and tinker on the piano. You see, Maurice didn't have money for piano lessons, [nor a piano]. He just had a desire to be in the church and learn to play an instrument. By tinkering on the

31

piano and watching other musicians, he taught himself how to play. Another gentleman in the neighborhood, who took interest in him, would buy him clothes when his family was not able to. Maurice, through all of that, taught himself not only to play the piano, but also to read music. With God's help and God's grace, he found himself in Washington, D.C., after growing up in Indiana, got a college education in Music Therapy, is a Registered Music Therapist, is now teaching at two Gospel Music Conventions, and is leading choirs and music programs at various churches around our nation.

It's because of the example - that Maurice has been - of a person who has been given things by God: Who has been given a talent by God, who has been given a heart to give – that I have encouraged him to write this book. Because I want the church to be edified and to know this is what God expects of his saints. Scripture tells us that the wealth of the wicked is stored up for the righteous. I believe that wealth is more than just physical and monetary things. I believe that wealth is the very spirit that wicked people refuse to share, i.e., the spirit of love, the spirit of joy, and [spirit of] happiness. Dr. Johnson is willing to do that. And because he has been willing to do that, he has become not only a godfather to countless, but has become a passionate preacher and [a] teacher of God's Holy word. Not only by speaking, but especially by doing!

The important thing about Maurice's story isn't what he has accomplished for himself, but rather in the legacy that he is already developing, which will far precede him after he is gone. Maurice has invested - his gifts, his talents, all that God has given him – into the lives of men and women, who call themselves…who are blessed to be called his godchildren. You will hear and read about some of them in this book. But, I've met some of them and I know [from which they have come].

Young men and women who didn't have much more than what Maurice had when he was growing up in Gary, Indiana. [These young people who were hopeless and saw no hope. Some wanted to attend college, but did not think they could]. Dr. Johnson has seen [to it] that they have gone to college. Not having transportation, he's helped them secure vehicles. Not having places to stay, he's opened his home to them. Sometimes, [they were] young men and women who were complete strangers! Yet, this man who came from nothing [and] who had nothing - reached out and pulled those up who had no place to go - and housed and fed them.

"DJ" has been a friend now, for almost 12-13 years. In that time, I've grown to know and love him like no other man that I've ever known in my life. My wife and my daughters count him as a very special member of our family. But it's not just been towards me, Herb. It's been his godchildren.

"To whom much is given, much is expected." (Paraphrased from Luke 12:48) The purpose for giving gifts and talents to men and women is to edify the Body of Christ, according to Romans 12 and I Corinthians 12. We are not to neglect the gifts that God has given us (See I Timothy) and we are to use our gifts to help one another (I Peter 4:10). Maurice has really been quite fortunate. God blessed him through the hands of several father figures. In turn, he has and continues to do the same for so many people.

D. Maurice Johnson

PART TWO

D. Maurice Johnson

`Eight

I met the young Miss Monique at Zion. She was a cute little two-year-old girl with her long hair done in pigtails on both sides of her head. For some reason we immediately took to each other. Whenever she saw me, she would take off running and would not stop until she had leaped into my arms. I had to pick her up and kiss her on the forehead before she would settle down. She followed my every move as long as I was in her presence. Also, I would always have to wipe her nose because it was always running. She hated that, but she eventually stopped resisting it because she had gotten used to it.

Monique was an only child being reared by her single mother. They shared a home with her maternal grandparents in Chicago. I knew her grandparents, her mother's siblings and all of their children because they also attended Zion. They all knew me, accepted me as her godfather, and referred to me by the special name that she used to called me, "Daddy D____." I was both pleased and honored that her mother endorsed our relationship, and hence supported and encouraged it.

Monique was a child of promise. She was educated in Catholic Schools and was a scholarly student who took her education very seriously. She consistently earned high grades. She had no trouble with articulation! She has always asked pointed questions, found answers to satisfy her curiosity, and honestly expressed her thoughts even if they left us feeling embarrassed or in awe. What really impressed me most about her was that she was courageous and adventuresome. She was always embarking upon some new venture at school. She left the security of her mother and their home to attend college in Wisconsin and later, study abroad in Italy.

There was a gap of several years in our interaction because she was doing her thing and I was doing mine. We may have talked to each other a few times per year, within a ten-year period. That is probably the reason that my description of her seems so minimal during her adolescent and early adulthood years of her life. We were both growing into the people that we have become today. Fortunately, our relationship was able to withstand the test of time and grow stronger, despite that period of limited interaction.

In the 1990's, we began to reestablish our relationship. Thank God, I am still her Dad or "Fatha", but not "Daddy D____." The primary thing we had to do was shift so that we related to each other as adults. She had matured to a college educated working professional even though she still lived at home. I had matriculated through college three times, and became a career professional who was married with a family. The shift was quite painless even though at times we felt uncomfortable setting boundaries with each other. The good thing about our current relationship is that there are no power struggles. We can reason with each other, listen objectively to each other's perspective and accept each other's perspective without animosity or being disagreeable. I have enjoyed the stimulating, and sometimes heated, discussions we have had regarding male and female relationships and behaviors that are gender specific.

Monique is strong-willed and determined yet, open-minded and flexible. Most of the time, she likes order and consistency in her environment. During her visits with me, her room turns into a disaster area, which drives me absolutely bonkers. She surprised me on her last visit. She did her usual: bags, clothes and shoes scattered everywhere. This time she did not wait for me to approach her. She just attended to her mess and disposed of the clutter. She made a point of showing me how her room was neat without my intervention. I was so pleased and humored by how she had handled my pet peeve.

She is very sensitive to the needs and concerns of others, sometimes going out of her way to appease the other person. She is thoughtful about the likes and dislikes of those she cares about. She has not lost her gift of articulating her thoughts, feelings and observations, which becomes more intense if they provoke her impatience. Even then, she still searches for tactful ways to approach her concerns. Overall, she is a kind-hearted and jovial person with a profound sense of humor and a wit to match.

Monique honors me by respecting my wisdom, sound judgment and counsel. She continues to allow me to protect, correct, nurture and support her as a loving father figure. I believe I honor her by celebrating her uniqueness, stimulating and encouraging her to accept new challenges, respecting her decisions and boundaries, and by telling and showing her that I love the person she has become. We have not forgotten the father-daughter aspect but rather, graduated to another level that factors the dynamic of friendship into the relationship equation. I am extremely proud of the very fine lady that my first and eldest goddaughter has become.

Nine

I met Master Leroy or "Baby brother" (pronounced Bay Bruh) when I moved on 19th Avenue in Gary. We both lived in the section called Tarrytown. He did not know it, but I already knew him because someone had told me all about him. This person lived in Tarrytown, attended school with Leroy, and she sang in the Youth choir at Tarrytown Baptist Church, where I was the Minister of Music. She told me his name, where he lived, and how he acted in school. Every morning and evening they walked past my home on their way to and from school. We met because he asked if he could cut my grass and wash my cars. He didn't' know that the only reason I agreed to let him do those things was because his friend had given me the low-down on the type of person he was.

We grew closer from our conversations. I found out he was a church boy. He regularly attended church with his mother. Although they were not very close, she always spoiled him and got him out of trouble when he needed to be rescued. His father only had minimal interaction with him. According to my musician friend, Leroy used to sing in the choir. From my friend, I found out that Leroy had already acquired a reputation for chasing the little "Nappy-headed" girls. His friend in my choir told me Leroy was an outstanding athlete. She was the one who kept me informed of his games, so that I could drop in on him unexpectedly and dip out before he knew I had been there.

Leroy eventually began to come to my house for visits, rather than to work. I can remember how surprised he was when I fed him for the first time. He could not believe that I could cook and bake so well. He said, "I like the way you cook. You can really burn!" During our visits I would inquire about the things that were going on in his life. For some reason, he never hesitated to be honest with me about what was happening. I sensed a closeness developing between us.

Leroy was a very bright and intelligent young man. But, the closer we got the more I realized how troubled Leroy really was about his home and school life. At home, he was getting into trouble doing things that kept him and his parents at odds. Needless to say, his troubles at school did not help their relationship either. His grades began slipping, he was getting suspended regularly, and he was not allowed to participate in school sports. I really began to get concerned about him when I noticed he was walking the streets at very odd times late at night. I used the things he shared with me as discussion starters regarding where he was emotionally. Despite all of his fine features and abilities, Leroy was quite troubled.

I think all of these things caused us to informally adopt each other. He would be so uptight that he would be on the verge of flicking off. After I quietly listened to him vent he would calm down. We would look at the events in his life from both perspectives without placing blame or judgment. Then we would discuss different ways to handle each one of the issues until we found a solution that he could live with. Each time we went through this process, he would later tell me that he had successfully dealt with each one. From those positive experiences he began to consider me like a father to him. He called me his God-Daddy in front of Greg, his friends, and other people in the neighborhood.

I think Leroy really was lost when I moved to Washington, D.C. One thing that was probably to his advantage was that he continued to maintain a relationship with Greg. So, we were able to maintain contact with each other. A couple of times he was at Greg's house when I called there. It was those times that

I could hear the loneliness in his voice. He would try to put up a brave front by telling me that he was OK, but my gut was telling me something different. Then I began getting calls from Greg and my other musician friend telling me about the negative things Leroy was doing. The most disturbing was that he was constantly getting high, drinking, and hanging out on the street corners. He never denied doing any of those things; but he also kept trying to reassure me that it was not as bad as I was led to believe. After several months of these conversations, I finally invited him to move to Washington, D.C. - to live. My conditions for him coming were that he would have to complete his high school education and get a job to support himself. He eagerly accepted the invitation and the conditions.

When Leroy arrived to Washington, D.C. he seemed to be both excited and relieved. I was happy and excited for him too. He saw how busy I was working the midnight shift as computer operator at George Washington University Hospital, attending classes all day at Howard University and playing for Greater Mount Zion in the evenings and ALL day on Sundays. He got right into the swing of things – He imitated me. He enrolled in G.E.D. classes, and school for Barbers at Armstrong Vocational, and worked in the evenings and on weekends at Hardees. He was really doing quite well. I was so proud of him. Less I mislead you, he still did some of those distracting "street things", but it was never in my presence. I never tried to control him. I just let him know that I was aware of what he was doing and reminded him of the reasons he was in Washington, D.C. with me. He accepted my observations and reminders without any angry discussion or argument.

In retrospect, I think Leroy took a turn for the worse when he realized I was moving to New Orleans to complete a Music Therapy internship program, and he had met a nice young lady.

He never said anything to me about how he really felt, but I saw his behavior began to change. They were inseparable. They were either on the phone, in the living room, or out socializing. Shortly afterward, she got pregnant. I was so furious that I did not know what to do! He already had two children back in Indiana. I tried to reason with him about the impact that another child and this relationship was going to have on his goals, but, for the first time ever he just tuned me out. That made me very angry because it hurt. I felt I was losing my ability to persuade him not to use poor judgment.

The move in 1992 was totally different from the other times. Leroy stayed for exactly one week! He would not even attempt to find work or enroll in school. Unless he went out partying with Robert, he would not leave the apartment. He just laid on a pallet in the living room watching TV all day long. I was so disappointed and frustrated with him. I tried not to pressure him or nag him, but even my calmest attempt to motivate him led to very heated arguments. It seemed as if all we did was argue! After one week he finally confided in me that he was concerned about his mother in recovery having a relapse. He was so convinced that his mother needed him that he decided to return to Gary. Against my objections and wisdom, I finally conceded to send him home. I was so outraged with him that we did not converse with each other for several months.

In February of the next year he called me to inform me that he had gotten into trouble, while hanging out in the streets, and had been sentenced to 15 years in prison on a trumped up charge. To this day, he claims he was a victim of mistaken identity and improper police protocol when he was arrested. I was very angry because he did not listen to me when I pleaded with him not to leave. I was even angrier for the price he had to pay for being in the wrong place at the wrong time, in "the streets!" He had been stripped of his freedom and his dignity shattered into a million fragments. His access to the love of his family, friends and loved ones was restricted.

What an awful price to pay! For five years Leroy was confined to inhumane physical (and mental) prison conditions and treated like a caged animal. No rights and no privileges! I agonized over what he had to experience. His imprisonment was devastating for all of us, but we managed to endure his plight only by our faith in God. It has truly been a painful labor of love to maintain our relationship. I *chose* to endure the expensive collect calls, to send and receive letters, to send postal money orders and care packages, and travel for hours (and miles) just to walk the dank, dark depressing prison halls. I became distressed during the long periods without any contact whatsoever, and hearing about his emotional state knowing that I could not say or do a thing to comfort him. Still, I *chose* to continue showing Leroy my love in tangible ways. Later he told me that what comforted him the most was he was confident in my love for him.

Every since Leroy has chosen me to be his Dad, he has been extremely protective of me. For example, if someone called me or answered my phone when he called, he immediately asks, "Who is this?" in a husky, demanding and intimidating voice. We have laughed about this because no one had to answer his question and because there was nothing he could do for me over the telephone from prison. He laughingly responded, "Yeah, I know, Dad. But, it made me feel better." [Thank you, son.]

It took time for us to make sense of his imprisonment and to iron out our differences. We had to honestly address the anger and resentment, the guilt and shame, the pain and hurt, and the agony and frustration. It has not been easy, or pleasant, but we have managed to get past all that. Now, we enjoy an even closer relationship because the incarceration has changed him for the better. He is less prone to react in anger, much more God-fearing and willing to be used as a servant of God. He has been actively involved in the ministry at the prison and pursuing an Associates Degree. He has focused on developing more meaningful positive and healthy relationships.

I am honored that Leroy respects my wisdom, judgment and counsel. He allowed me to lovingly protect, correct, nurture and support him as his father figure. I honor him when I celebrate his uniqueness; stimulate and encourage him to accept new challenges, respect his decisions and boundaries, and demonstrate my love with words reinforced by deeds. Just as with Monique, we have factored the dynamic of friendship into our relationship. I am extremely proud of the very fine man that my first and eldest godson has become.

Ten

I met Miss Iisha in 1990 at Gethsemane Baptist Church in Washington, D.C. where I was serving as the Minister of Music. She sang in the Young People's Choir. For some reason this 13 year-old young lady used to constantly hang around my office. Between the 8:00 a.m. and 11:00 a.m. services she would come to my office to inquire if I needed anything done. She would also go to the fellowship hall to get breakfast for me.

I was quite familiar with Iisha's family because they were members of Gethsemane as well. Iisha was the oldest child in her family. Her family consisted of her mother, stepfather, and a younger sister. Her maternal grandmother was also a very dominating influence in their lives. She had very strong negative feelings regarding her family, with the exception of her sister. She resented the way she was treated by her mother and grandmother, and she despised her stepfather. She was chronically frustrated about her interactions with them, or the lack of healthy interaction with them. Her mother and I had several conversations about how they related. She gave me the impression that she was appreciative and receptive to my observations and suggestions, but I later realized that she resented my interventions and seldom gave much credence to any of the suggestions that I had offered. Iisha knew who her biological father was, but never had any real interaction with him. According to Iisha, her biological and stepfather were insignificant to her.

As time progressed, we began to get closer. She told me that she considered me to be like a dad to her. Then, she began to refer to me as daddy, which was ok with me. To this day I am not sure how her mother or grandmother really felt about this, but everyone in the church knew and accepted our relationship.

We have had numerous "serious" talks about things that were important to her, i.e., her relationship with her family, school issues and things that were happening among the members of her choir. She would talk and I would listen. Then, if she asked, I would offer suggestions for approaching the challenges that she was facing. Iisha was a very angry young teenager with a very serious attitude and a tongue that was brutal. What we discovered was that most times, her responses were on the mark, but she had great difficulty being expressive without being disrespectful or hurtful. I think she had grown so accustomed to experiencing these types of responses that she adopted them as her own style of relating to other people. Because of the role she had assigned to me, I began to coach her on how to appropriately express her thoughts and feelings. In every instance she had to report back to me with the outcome of her efforts. Even though she was typically reluctant or resistant, she always heeded my suggestions and was surprised when she got positive results. She gradually began to trust my wisdom and respect my judgment, but not without an initial bout of opposition! Fortunately, we were still able to bond because we related to each other quite well. She knew quite well that I held her accountable for her actions, speech and attitude!

She was a good student with a bright mind and sharp wit. She studied regularly even though she always achieved good grades whether or not she had studied. She would bring copies of her report cards and test papers for me to keep. For the most part, she was progressing very well, despite her frustration regarding her tense relationship with her mother and stepfather. During her junior year of high school her grades dropped in several important subjects. Her mother responded by punishing her, which meant she could not participate in any church activities. With great difficulty, I was eventually able to help Iisha understand what was going on from a parental perspective. She did not like what she heard but she accepted my feedback. Another thing that she was forced to deal with was my stance regarding her mother's wishes. I consistently reinforced what her mother expected of her, whether she liked it or not. The next grading period her grades had improved drastically. She later admitted that she had not been applying herself. She was talking on the telephone rather than doing homework and studying.

Iisha was really excited when she got her first job at Burger King. She surprised me because she was able to maintain a job without neglecting her studies. I do not know how she did it, but she simultaneously juggled school, her studies, her job and her late night phone conversations. One good thing that happened was she was learning how to drive and being given driving privileges. Now my visits with her were not restricted to church or her home, she was able to come to visit me at my home. She had found a place that was safe to her and developed an even stronger sense of belonging with me. She hated that she had to limit her visits because I had housemates, one of which was my other godson, Willie. After Willie went away to college and the house was cleared of all roommates, I gave her a key to the house. She immediately staked her claim to one of the bedrooms. She did not like it when she had to return the key, a few years later, because I was planning to get married to a woman with two young children. More about that later....

I was so proud of Iisha when she graduated from high school. She had chosen to attend college in North Carolina. It was a good experience for her because she learned, and did, so many things in a hurry. First, she had the opportunity to live away from home for the first time as an independent adult, which meant she had to decide the direction that she wanted her life to go. She had to cope with meeting financial obligations and exercise good judgment regarding her spending. She quickly learned to distinguish between needs and wants. In addition, she was forced to accept the reality that supporting her lifestyle was her responsibility, not the responsibility of someone else. She worked the entire school year and every summer. I laughed inwardly when she told me, "Daddy, I really don't want to work, but I need money. I've got bills to pay!" [Good for you, Baby!]

Second, she was learning more about how to relate with others appropriately. She managed to maintain a long distance relationship with her high school sweetheart who was attending college in Atlanta, while simultaneously dealing with new guys who she found attractive or that found her attractive. She met new students and personalities in her classes and while working on campus. Everyone on campus knew who she was. During my many visits, I was proud to hear from the students and faculty that she was quite likeable, renowned, popular and well-mannered.

A part of her learning about relationships happened when she pledged a sorority. I was concerned that joining a sorority would distract her from her studies and lower her Grade Point Average. And it did! I was also concerned about the awful beating and abuse or "hazing" that reportedly occurs on all college campuses. Watching these various types of abuses that are prevalent nationwide on the Oprah Winfrey Show only helped to intensify my concern. Then, hearing the agony, despair and pain in Iisha's voice when she called did not help either. I finally went to put an end to that madness! They were either going to find other non-threatening ways to haze Iisha or I was going to report them to their National Office. Needless to

49

say, I allowed Iisha to talk me out of what I had intended. When she finally "crossed the burning sand" (became a member) I let out a huge sigh of relief. In retrospect, pledging was a good thing! Iisha was forced to respect authority and boundaries and to accept her inability to control persons and situations. She also gained a clearer self-concept and identity while establishing a brand new network of resources that would be at her disposal for the rest of her life.

Another part of her learning about relationships happened when she decided to drop out of college and return to Maryland to pursue a new relationship. Her mother and grandmother were furious and extremely disappointed! So was I! Iisha tried to reassure me that she would continue her education when she returned home. I desperately tried many times to persuade her to reconsider, but she had already proceeded with her plans. Reluctantly, I respected her decision even though I did not agree with it. While simultaneously pursuing that relationship, she worked a temporary job that came in handy when she was forced to move out of the house with her mother. Fortunately, I was able to get her an apartment in my name because she was offered a job in a permanent editorial position. Things seemed to appear as if they were going great for Iisha. But the longer she stayed in that relationship the more uncomfortable Sean ("Uncle Sean") and I became. That relationship became the focal point of her life. They were abusive, controlling, manipulative and possessive of each other. I frequently made them angry because I pointed out my concerns every time I got the chance. My comments were only intended to be helpful but they seemed to push her farther away from me. Our conversations became more infrequent and strained. Rather than continue to hinder our relationship, I decided to keep my observations and counsel to myself.

Gradually, they both began to seek me whenever troublesome situations arose. I was careful to respond objectively. I also made sure that I was impartial when it came to accountability. I went to great lengths to make sure that they knew I was attempting to offer them rational wisdom without any judgment. I presented my responses as suggestions using many different scenarios as options. In some cases it worked, but in other instances they just blew me off. It was just a matter of time that the dramatic behaviors became so unbearable that the relationship was abruptly terminated. Iisha told me she felt abandoned and utterly devastated. It was a good thing that she was able to hear the counsel she received from a private therapist and her "Daddy-therapist." The conclusion of that relationship marked a real turning point in her life.

It was difficult for Iisha to accept the fact that I was getting married. She knew my fiancée, but she did not want me to marry her. She had so many reservations and concerns. She frequently reminds me that she had every intention of hitting me over the head with a stick to knock me out on my wedding day. She alleges the only reason she did not was because Uncle Keith and Herb stopped her. She did not like my wife, but she adored my two stepchildren. However, I adamantly insisted that she respect my new family and their rights. She had no choice in the matter! As usual, she complied but she sure did not like it. Iisha later told me that my wife never treated her like a daughter, she only used her as a babysitter or to influence me to respond affirmatively for what she wanted. My interaction with Iisha during that period was limited: partly because of her dislike for my wife, but also because she was caught up in her own unhealthy relationship.

When my marriage fell apart, Iisha was with me every step of the way. She saw my tears, pain, and shame, but she also

51

heard my anger and frustration. She acted as a buffer during the crisis stage, i.e., she was there to comfort me and protect me. She made sure my wife and I had no contact with each other. Several months later, we briefly fell out because she finally admitted that she could not understand why I responded the way that I did when she initially pretended to understand. I think it was a woman thing! Anyway, somehow we managed to work our way through the angry feelings and find our way back to each other. When we did reconcile, she was even more of a "mother hen" than she was before. She was at every court hearing with me. Just recently she admitted that she had worried about me during the entire 2-year divorce process.

I am very proud of the effort that Iisha has demonstrated toward her personal maturation. Iisha has survived several complex, major transitions in her life. She has come a long way in her development and ability to relate to others. She was forced to look at the destructive nature of her "learned" behavior and speech while finding new ways to establish and maintain healthy meaningful relationships. But, open communication and conflict resolution are still major challenges that she must conquer. She created a new identity as a result of her previous relationship. She had been promoted to managing editor, earned a bachelor's degree in Journalism, purchased her first car, and engaged in a new meaningful relationship that she cherishes. I should mention that between the first relationship that I mentioned and this new one, she attempted and terminated two other ones because she concluded they were not healthy for her. [Good for you, Baby!] The only way Iisha can be sure about who she is and what she likes is by doing what is common to all young adults: exploring, experimenting, evaluating and adjusting.

Iisha and I enjoy a unique relationship. I am her Daddy-Friend and she is my Daughter-Friend. She gets miserable if we do not talk to each other at least once a day, and she gets even more miserable if we do not see each other for several days. **[Confession time...sometimes I do too!]** We have keys to each other's place of residence. If she comes over when I am out she brings in the mail. And, God-forbid if the phone rings. She makes a mad dash to answer it, even if I am at home! Today, we are still working on boundary issues, especially her answering my telephone. When I go over to her apartment, I practice the same rules at her place as she has at mine. By the way, she does comply but she hates them! We talk about everything. We give each other "gas" but we love each other very much.

When she gets on my nerves, I refer to Iisha as my "mother." Iisha is very selfish, protective, and caring when it comes to me. She has had conflicts on several different occasions with different people who are close to me because she has felt threatened by their relationship to me, e.g., my wife, Willie, and Monique. I have had to reassure her of her "eternal" special place in my heart, and that my heart is big enough to have similar places for others who also want to share in my life just as she does. I think she's beginning to feel more comfortable with that. Then, she does not like me living alone and she thinks I do not eat or sleep properly. She wants to know where I am and with whom. I usually just ignore her, laugh at her, or placate her. Sometimes I do have to ask her, "How did I survive all these years without you?" She loves to boss me around, which is her way of showing me that she loves me. If she knows that I am not feeling well or tired or unavailable, she calls. If she gets really worried, she'll ask, "Daddy, are you ok?

You sure?" When I confront her she says, "But Daddy, ...you love me."

[My daughters are good at deflecting- they simply toss the word "love" in the situation.]

Iisha honors me by listening to my wisdom, sound judgment and counsel. She accepts my love, support, protection, correction, and nurture because in her eyes I am her only father figure! I accept and respect her, stimulate and encourage her to accept new challenges, and reassure her (by word and deed) how important she is to me. Iisha has blossomed into a very fine young woman. It makes me even prouder when she exercises good judgment - in advance.

Eleven

In 1993, I worked at a high school in Washington, D.C. as a permanent substitute teacher. Part of my duties was to monitor the halls and keep them clear of students. There were several incidents where I encountered this very angry young man that I always managed to calm down and persuade to return to class. I asked what his name was after redirecting him on several occasions. It was Willie Lawson. The encounters seemed to occur frequently, so I asked what was troubling him. He always told me. Sometimes the troubles were academic, other times they were about faculty or students, and other times they were personal. But, one thing always remained constant – Willie went into an out-of-control rage whenever he was troubled. His explosions were really about sour relationships.

I really had no idea how much Willie had been struggling just to survive until I was asked to direct the Gospel Choir. He had a strong interest in music and even though he was not the greatest singer, he loved to sing. For our first performance the choir was to wear black and white attire. A faculty member informed me that Willie wanted to perform but did not have very many clothes, especially black and white. He graciously accepted my offer to purchase the items for him, which meant we had to go shopping. That brief shopping trip was very enlightening for me! I began to understand why this 16 year-old young man was so troubled.

Willie was living in a transitional home, which was intended to prepare kids to live on their own. Most of the residents in this home had lived on the streets, had been through the legal system, and were either on probation or in a counseling program. Willie had been living on the streets since he was thirteen years old. His family consisted of his mother, stepfather, and three brothers. He was the second oldest child. I could see the pain in his eyes as he told me about his family life. He told me that he always felt like he was the "black sheep" of his family. He claimed they treated him as if his needs and feelings did not matter, nor were they a priority. He rebelled at the neglect, which left him out on the streets. He lived from place-to-place in the homes of others, adopted the fast pace of the streets and "caught charges" in the legal system. I could not believe what he had to contend with just to survive! It was a wonder that he was even able to make it to school with any regularity, not to mention function academically. No child should have to deal with such things and be expected to matriculate through high school. After we had finished shopping, I fed him and took him to the place where he was staying.

I continued to interact with Willie at school, especially during choir rehearsals. I began to know and understand him better. In essence, I saw his heart. Then, my quiet inner concern regarding Willie's living situation took on a personality of its own. I was so vexed that I prayed about it and discussed it with my housemate, Robert. He was reluctant, but eventually agreed to let Willie stay with us during the week until he finished high school.

I asked Willie for permission to show him some things that would help him be a more positive young man. He accepted my offer, but neither one of us knew what we were getting ourselves into. We were both students. Willie was attending high school and I was working on a Doctor of Ministry Degree in the Seminary. We spent quite a bit of time together. We rode to school together, talked about life issues and relationships, watched TV and movies, did homework, and really bonded. He began to refer to me as his god-dad, because he felt I was like a father to him, which was fine with me. He also called me "pops", "DJ" or just "D." I was so proud to see that his family, and even his friends and even the faculty endorsed our relationship.

I soon learned that Willie was a charming passionate person, a bright student, and a music lover. He made good grades without studying and he learned fast. He had an inquisitive mind that made him quite persistent and demanding at times. On the other hand, he easily became enraged, rebelled against authority, and pushed boundaries to the limit. I never liked how he treated his girlfriends! He thought he could beat them into submission. To me, he was acting like their father. He had a unique perspective on things, which he thought was logical, and expected things to flow according to that perspective without regard for the consequences or the "residue." He knew that I was observing him very closely because my area of study was pastoral care in youth ministry. He often told me that he hated when I analyzed him because he was not a part of my research. But I learned so much about teens from him.

Willie and Robert had a hard time adjusting to each other. Robert worked as a counselor with children at a mental hospital. He was quite comfortable with children but Willie presented him with challenges that he was not able to deal with. Robert wanted to counsel him and Willie rejected his efforts. Willie resented Robert's counsel because they seemed childlike to him. He said Robert did not invest any time in developing a relationship with him. But, I observed how much they had really grown to care about each other. Neither one of them admitted it to the other, but I could sense their care and concern for each other. Robert got gravely ill before Willie graduated from high school. He was hospitalized for a month and placed in a nursing home for several weeks. Willie knew that I was spending all my time caring for Robert, but he would never visit him in the hospital. He did visit the nursing home when they informed me Robert would not make it through the night. He tried to put on a brave front while we were there but he broke into tears as soon as we got in the car. He bravely and quietly supported me through that entire ordeal. Robert made me promise on his deathbed that I would give Willie his Black Nissan Pulsar.

Willie graduated from high school. Thank God! He was not sure whether he wanted to work or attend college. He talked about being a Band Teacher and writing books that would help young people. He could not decide whether he wanted to attend college in the District of Columbia or Daytona Beach, Florida. After months of indecisiveness he selected Florida two weeks before classes began. He made his decision while I was out of town teaching for two weeks at the annual Gospel Music conventions. I began getting him prepared as soon as I returned home. I made so many phone calls and faxed so many documents that he was accepted within several days. Willie passed the SAT exam without studying! His ability to do that really reinforced my belief that he could do whatever he wanted to if he tried. Willie was so excited when we flew to Florida the following week. That was his first airplane ride!

Willie very quickly settled in, but his stay was tenuous. He got over being homesick once he felt the demands of classes and the marching band. He made some new friends in the dormitory that he lived in. I knew Willie's temperament and perspective would get him in trouble so I asked the Dean to call me personally if problems arose. Willie called me after a month because he was in trouble, then I began to get calls from the Dean of Students. He eventually got sent home for his destructive behavior, which he claimed was a rebellion for the poor living conditions in the dormitory. I was so very disappointed that he did not achieve his goal.

We decided that Willie would take some time to regroup from his first college experience. I had only intended for it to last a few weeks, but he had something else in mind. He half-heartedly attempted to find work, but he still wanted to live and be entertained at my expense. He found numerous weak reasons why he could not find work. I kept my promise to look out for him and to make sure that he took possession of the black Nissan Pulsar. He enjoyed the respite, but I had grown intolerant with his slothful attitude toward work or completing projects that he started. He grew intolerant with my nagging so we argued a lot! I set new boundaries, confronted him for not doing his part, and took away his key to the house and phone privileges. Initially, he tried to be respectful when he was angry by not talking or leaving the room. I had to help him understand I was not afraid of his anger. Our biggest problem was being clear about what we felt, needed, and expected from each other. Another problem was how we presented our concerns to each other. We became closer because we worked through those really frustrating times.

Willie had great difficulty because he loved the benefits of a nice suburban lifestyle, but he was driven by the habits he had acquired in the streets. He wanted them to coexist simultaneously. He would make attempts toward growth but quickly retreated to "street" behavior whenever he got rejected or frustrated. He wanted to do the positive things that he dreamed about but he did not seem to have the perseverance to allow them to materialize. According to him, it was quicker, easier and less of a hassle to do things the street way. Many times he got hurt or abused while trying to be loyal to his friends in the street.

We tried the college thing one more time. This time he drove the Pulsar to Florida against my repeated warnings not to do so. He attended classes with a new determination for a while. But, true to form, he got expelled after a short time. He had also wrecked the car and abandoned it in Florida. If I am not mistaken, he remained in Florida to work for several months before he returned home. I was happy to see him when I picked him up from the airport, but I was disappointed that he had gotten sent home a second time. Also, I was (and still am) angry that he was so nonchalant about the car Robert had bequeathed to him. This time he did not get a respite; he only had a few days to get a job. He was a little more determined but he never achieved his goal. This time there were not any arguments from me just friendly reminders. I was trying to be patient and supportive but my tolerance was completely gone. It finally got to the point when I had to ask him to move out of my house. I had attempted this several times before but I always seemed to acquiesce. He moved in with his cousin for a while but moved out when he met this young woman. That is another story in itself.

I really did not see or hear that much from Willie for a while after he moved out. I was angry about his choices and the lifestyle he wanted to live. I would call his cousin's apartment, when the phone was working, but he would be over his lady's house. He had moved in with her and her young son. I respected him for trying to establish his own household. He was still mixing it up in the street, but I did not interfere. As a matter of fact, I was practically scarce. Then, there was a long period of time that I did not know how to reach him because they had moved to a place with no phone. When he finally did show me where he lived it was worse than before, which really worried me so I stayed away unless he asked me to visit. He and his lady experienced some interactions that led to his incarceration on several different occasions.

I have been to the courts and jails to see him so much that I despise them! Every visit broke my heart each time. I repeatedly reminded him that he was no criminal and that a dehumanizing place was not where he needed to be spending his young vital life. He had been fortunate because his sentences had been short. But the last time, he spent nearly a year in jail because of who he was around and being in the streets. I was so angry with him that I did not even let him tell me what happened as I usually would. Instead, I refused his phone calls and did not visit him for nearly six months. We had some very harsh things to say to each other before we were able to begin the process of reconciliation.

In between the first jail sentence and the last sentence I got married. Willie was fond of my fiancée and her two children. He had encouraged me to pursue a nice woman to be my mate, so he was glad to be a part of the wedding. It was Willie who first observed she was after me. Also, he gave me his perspectives (unsolicited and solicited) on how I should deal with her during our relationship. We developed an even deeper bond during this time because we were both in relationships with women we considered significant others and who had children. We talked quite a bit about male-female relationships, child rearing, and gender roles in the biblical perspective of marriage. When my marriage ended he was very supportive. He came when I called and checked on me more frequently. His presence from the break up through the divorce was a source of great comfort. In retrospect, Willie has consistently been there to comfort me. He was also with me the day I learned that my mother had died. [Thanks, son.] Willie was beginning to feel the brutal nature of adulthood in the real world.

Then, the same tumultuous relationship that caused him to be imprisoned yet another time, ended while he was locked up. Regretfully, I was not there to comfort him. The subsequent reconciliation process was difficult but true to form, we worked through it and learned from it. The events of the last few years forced us both to mature and gain new perspectives of each other. We are different people than we were before. I have since acknowledged that while Willie is like a son to me, he is a grown man. And because he is a grown man, Willie must make his own choices whether I agree with them or not. In addition, the consequences of his choices belong to him as well. Our relationship has become much closer and even more meaningful since I have decided to see him from this perspective.

Willie respects my wisdom, sound judgment and counsel most times. He likes to make me think he is not listening, but at a later time he says or does something that shows me he has taken every single word to heart. He reluctantly continues to allow me to protect, correct, nurture and support him as loving father figure when it is convenient. He still struggles with wanting me to rescue him from his own misfortunes. WRONG! I try to listen objectively seeking to understand him, offer him a few different perspectives and options, stimulate and encourage him to accept new challenges, respect his decisions and boundaries (reluctantly, when I foresee a harmful outcome). I am intentional about giving him a balanced dose of praise and rebuffs in order to reinforce the point that my love toward him is constant regardless to the situation or what appears to be reality. Part of me is proud of the fine young man that he is becoming, and happy about the friendship dynamic in our relationship. However, my fatherly instincts are screaming out at me, "Willie really needs firm boundaries and clear direction from me as his father figure. [I'm there son, and I got ya.]

It feels like it has taken me longer to parent Willie, than all of my other children. Is that because we have both grown older? Or am I just imagining this in my mind? Hmmmm????

Twelve

Ms. Christina was one of the first young people that I met at Highland Hills UMC in Dallas, Texas. She was a pleasant, warm and charming young lady. She was also very committed, faithful and eager to participate in the activities that brought us together. What I found to be impressive was that many times she was at the church before anyone else arrived at the church, including me. I found out later that most times she would have taken the bus to the church directly from school and spent several hours there waiting for the rest of us to arrive. Also, she would call me in advance if she knew she was going to be absent. If something that was beyond her control happened and she was not able to make the call in advance, she would call me later to inform me of what had happened. She was very dependable.

Chris and I got close because she always made herself available to assist me in whatever ways she could. She would call choir members for me, make copies for me or get things that I needed for whatever we were doing. Needless to say, she was always around me at the church. There were times that she asked me to give her a ride home. She would wait around patiently until I finished the things that I needed to do, which meant we were usually the last ones to leave the premises. If I did not have things for her to do, she worked on her homework or sat quietly while I did what I needed to do.

The times we spent together made a tremendous impact on our relationship. We got a chance to know each other on a deeper level and to understand each other in ways that helped us both to grow as friends and as struggling Christians in our journeys toward spiritual maturity. We talked about everything, i.e., things that were funny and sad, good and bad, pleasant and painful.

I learned about her immediate family, circle of friends, school life and church life during our numerous rides to her home in a new housing development in the nearby suburban of Mesquite, Texas. She was the middle child in her family that consisted of her parents, an older sister and a younger brother. Her parents were not members of our church. Her mother was a member of another church in Dallas and her father seldom attended church. We became acquainted with each other because we interacted whenever I drove her home or they picked her up. She was very close to her mother and sister, and very protective and nurturing to her brother. She painfully spoke of her desire for a much closer relationship with her father on numerous occasions.

She claimed to be close with only a few people. She had a very strong character and was easily turned off by peers who were negative, pretentious, or immoral. She was very serious about her studies and tended to stay away from people who were not like-minded. She was a creative artist and quite computer literate. I was so amazed by the beautiful work she brought to show me, which she also had compiled into a neat little portfolio. Much of her artwork was displayed around the church and used for church programs.

I often heard reports that she was considered a likable and out-going person at school and church. She was fun to be around and funny! I liked how she was very active in our Junior-Senior High Sunday school class. She was eager about God, the word of God and her spirituality. She asked the hard questions and struggled to find and apply scriptural answers to her problems in her daily life. One day in class she asked, "How come when we have problems the adults in church tell us

65

to go pray? They don't show us, they all just assume that we know how to pray!" Her stance was so very profound and provocative that I have never forgotten it to this day. It was apparent to me that she wanted to apply one of the fundamental Christian tenets to her personal situation in life, but she was struggling because no adult Christian had taken the time to teach her how to do what they had prescribed as an intervention. Needless to say, our class devoted much more time learning and practicing how to pray. She pricked my interest in Christian Education. I think of her every time, I train teachers and lecture in method classes.

During the time Chris was asking this question, her parents marriage began to deteriorate. She was having difficulty accepting the fact that her family was not an ideal one. When her parents finally divorced, she was forced into a new living arrangement that she resented because her familiar comfortable lifestyle had suddenly become unfamiliar and certainly unpredictable. It took a lot of tears, conversations, and assurances to help her through that traumatic period in her life.

Shortly after that transition Chris had to deal with high school graduation and the college selection process. Surprisingly, she rose to the occasion with little anguish. Her biggest struggle was deciding to attend an out-of-state college. She did not want to leave her mother with the responsibility of being alone to care for her and her younger brother. Somehow her mother must have convinced her to do what was best for her because Chris chose to attend a college in Indiana.

We remained in contact with each other while she was attending college. In phone calls and letters she would tell me how difficult it was for her to be so far away from her mother and from me. She told me her contact with us is what kept her sane. She matriculated through several years of college with high grade point averages, but she also experienced the usual worries about the long drives to and from school, the exams, finances, and social life. I thought she was doing a fantastic job of coping with all the things she had to cope with. It pleased her to hear me praise her many accomplishments.

The real challenge was when Chris decided to join a chapter of an African American Sorority that did not exist at her predominantly European American College. She faced so much resistance and so many restrictions that she was ready to trash the whole venture. She hung in there until she managed to get the chapter established. But it happened only after countless hours of encouraging phone conversations and the influence of several unexpected political resources on campus. She was so very proud of what she had accomplished. I was proud too! I watched her goal become a reality through sheer perseverance, determination and diligence. This child of such great promise finished the semester flying high. And she deserved every bit of it!

Chris had a good summer that year. She was finally adjusting to her mother's new living arrangement, her maternal family was being very supportive, and she had gotten a good summer job that she really liked. She was excited about going back to college in the fall. We talked on the telephone the week before she was to return to school, but we didn't talk for several weeks after that. I was so surprised when I got a call from her mother that following week. During that conversation she told me that Chris and her aunt were in a car accident while taking her back to school. Neither of them survived the accident. I was so stunned and heartbroken that I just sat there speechless with tears streaming down my face. I struggled as best I could to be emotionless while her mother was on the telephone, but the pain of Chris' death (and my loss) had suddenly pierced my heart and shattered it into a million pieces. A few weeks later I felt the same pain when I received a copy of the obituary in the mail from her mother. I was saddened that her young life had ended so abruptly.

In her own special way, Chris unknowingly provoked me into Youth Ministry. She made me aware that I had a passion for helping young people begin to see themselves as Christians and humans. From our genuine relationship, I begin to understand youth as unique, valuable, capable, productive, and essential persons to the life of our families, churches, communities and the world. Most of all, I have learned how much teens need adults to love, care, and nurture them as they struggle to live spiritual and meaningful lives. They need us to help them endure the chronic changes of adolescence and to equip them to make the painful transition from dependent children to independent adults.

Chris taught me that youth need to practice what they have been told and shown by adults. We have a responsibility to make sure that they are not deprived of that opportunity and that they have a safe environment to begin making the adjustments necessary to integrate the "adult things" into their own lifestyles, worldview and belief system. They need us to let them practice on us in every sense of the term. I mean practice being adult, autonomous, independent, spiritual, Christian and any other descriptor that you can imagine – We must give them room to refine what we have taught them with our loving guidance.

What is inevitable is that trial and error, or practice, is a natural part of the process by which they achieve healthy growth and development. We both grew and developed while relating to each other. Unbeknownst to her, she influenced and motivated me to pursue doctoral studies in pastoral care and youth ministry in non-traditional and non-clinical settings, because my primary interest was on relationship, rather than the place and protocol.

Thirteen

It was my first meeting with the youth choir at Highland Hills United Methodist Church (UMC). Each youth was asked to indicate their name and what vocal part they sang. One young man, who stood over 6 feet tall, spoke at a volume level that was so low, I could barely hear what he had said. He was a tenor named David.

David and his younger sister lived with his maternal grandmother, their legal guardian, on the street directly behind the church. I often wondered about his parents, but he never mentioned them so I never asked. His aunt and her son knew me because they were active members of the church. They made it possible for me to learn more about David and his family.

David struck me as a low-key kind of boy. He was reserved, polite, courteous, easy-going and even-tempered. Initially, I had perceived him as a bashful person, but over time he showed me that he was very faithful. I seldom had to wonder about David being present because he was rarely absent. He was not the best singer but he certainly was loyal to the choir. The same was true regarding our Junior/Senior High Sunday school class. He was not the most active or outspoken student, but he was always there sitting quietly or smiling. I could count on David when all others failed.

It took quite some time to engage David. His low-key emotionless persona allowed him to blend into situations and settings just like all other "cool" guys. He did what was expected of him. He never uttered angry words or needed correction. The more I knew him the more I really liked David, the person. He was mindful of his place yet, sensitive to the needs of others. He was kind and a gentle giant with a great big, caring heart. He was always so willing and eager to help others, even when he did not feel good himself.

As time progressed, we talked more. I could sense the deep sadness that his persona and quietness were trying to conceal. I felt so very bad that such a wonderful boy was hurting so deep down on the inside. My instincts were screaming out for me to gently nurture him. That is when I decided to initiate a closer relationship with David. I discussed my intention with the pastor, his aunt, his grandmother and him. Every one of them thought it was a good idea, especially David. I really desired to help this young man feel better and experience some new joyful memories. We grew closer by spending time together at church, on the telephone, or at the mall. In retrospect, I chose to nurture David because he really was a good kid who needed some adult male interaction, a male with whom he could feel like he belonged. For example, "joning" or making fun of peers is a part of how youth tend to socialize, so if I caught him occasionally snickering while others were "joning" I would have to force myself to give him a very mild rebuff. I was merely fulfilling my role as his gentle but firm nurturer.

During his last year of high school, David was having great anxiety about his grades and graduation. I really surprised him the day I showed up at his school unannounced to get my own perspective on what was happening. He was so proud to introduce me as his godfather to his teachers and his peers. He later told me how pleased he was to have someone, besides his grandmother, take the time to come see about him. He felt like he was special and that he mattered to someone. He was special and he did matter!

During the last semester of David's senior year, things changed quite radically. I had resigned from Highland Hills and was also preparing for my own graduation. He was preparing

71

for graduation and all the ceremonial festivities related to graduation. We did not get to spend much time together or on the phone. We both graduated. David moved to Arizona and I returned to Washington, DC. We remained in contact with each other for a while but eventually lost contact for many years. I was very saddened to learn of David's death from his cousin a few years ago. His cousin is pleased about David's legacy and believes David's son can now get an idea of what kind of man his father was. Well, David Jr. I hope this helps. In memory of your father, David Sr., the "gentle giant," I challenge you to be like your father and to use your love to make someone else blossom.

From David I learned that real love and respect are gifts to be treasured. It is our responsibility to recognize them as such, hold them dear to us, and share them with others. In his own special and quiet way David showed how much he really appreciated the love and support he received from me. Also, he was a testimony of how love makes a person blossom - grow and develop into a normal, healthy, productive human being. David granted me the honor of showering him with a fatherly kind of love that empowered him to grow. It was my privilege to have shared with him and to have witnessed his growth. I am so very proud of David and his accomplishments. As Keith says, "I love to see young lions roar! That's what David did! He roared and soared leaving a wonderful memory for us to cherish forever.

PART THREE

D. Maurice Johnson

*"And you shall love the Lord your God with all your heart, and
with all your soul,
and with all your might. And these words, which I command you
this day shall
be upon your heart; and you shall teach them diligently to your
children, and
shall talk of them when you sit in your house, and when you walk
by the way,
and when you lie down, and when you rise."* Deuteronomy 6:5-7

The gospel according to my little "play" brother, Sean is this: "Much of what is written here you will probably identify with in your own life. We all know that there are times when, as biological or substitute parents, we can influence our children by being there for them, by listening to them, and by helping them in their times of growth and struggles. And of course, there are times when we must step back and allow them to go through their experiences on their own. But, not so far back that we don't allow them to share their experiences. And not so far back that we, as parents don't share our experiences together as a family. It is true that unless you are able to talk to each other openly and honestly, the ability for both the child and parent to move to a higher level of growth will either not occur or will be stunted. This kind of mutual sharing must always occur and be done with love."

Sean continues: "Even if you do not have your own children, always remember: "We are still part of a village. And every child that you will come across is also your child!" A good metaphor for this is when Jesus fed the multitudes (his children) with five barley loaves and two fish (Matthew 14:19, Luke 9:13, John 6:11). You must also feed your children (our children) with your love, guidance, knowledge and experience."

Fourteen

I believe I am "DJ's" first, but not the oldest, Godchild. My first memory of him is from the Zion Missionary Baptist Church in East Chicago. I don't know what it was about "DJ" that made me want to follow him around Zion all the time. It could have been his personality or it could have been his love for music, which I also shared at a very young age.

"DJ" was unlike any other adult, including my mother. In the sense that he was not pushing anyone away. He was a very social person. I remember the "old" Zion Church with its very hard benches that hurt your behind when you sat down. You couldn't get comfortable if you tried! I would sit next to him on the organ while he was playing and he would let me turn that On/Off switch. Do you know to this day I still don't know what that On/Off switch did for the organ? I just know that it was important to turn it every so often. (She is referring to the Leslie switch on Hammond Organs.) I used to sit there, watch him play; watch the church and press the switch, basically. Now of course, "DJ" wants me to mention the second part of the story and that is, when it was time for the sermon, I would crawl in his lap and fall asleep. Now since we're going back over twenty something years, I have to say that I don't remember that, necessarily. But I can believe it, because I am a child that loves to sleep during the sermon instead of listening to them.

I remember wanting to learn how to play the piano just like him. So, I took piano lessons. Maybe the teacher just wasn't as aggressive or supportive, I don't know, but I just remember losing interest very quickly. Which, somehow or another, my interest changed and I developed the interest for singing. Not realizing that, *believe or not*, Yes, I can sing. *I know that probably surprises you.* For some reason, I feel really uncomfortable with attention on me, so that causes me not to want to sing in public, except singing in the shower and crazy stuff like that. Singing while I'm cleaning. Maybe it's just something personal, that "DJ" and I share…music. I just don't wish to share with everyone. I might be selfish. I won't deny that.

"DJ" and I have known each other for a long time. He has been a friend, and my father; always supportive of the things I wanted to do; and telling me that I could do them, which takes nothing away from my relationship with my mother. There are certain things that mothers do not understand, but fathers do, and DJ did. My need to be independent, my need to grow; my need to stand-alone. I'm realizing today, how much alike we really are.

There was a time in our lives when we were not keeping in touch. I always knew where he was, but I could probably give you an excuse; but it's pointless. I just didn't keep in touch with him. Maybe there were other things going on in my life…but that is not an excuse. I am glad, however, that I've re-established my relationship with my Godfather, because I've realized how important it was to me! We're both very strong individuals (sometimes…well, he's stubborn, I'm just self-confident). But I know we love each other.

It's just amazing how God has put certain people in our lives, extended family I'm talking about, to help move us along - to give us that push in the right direction. For some reason my family has never supported me the way a family should. My mother and grandfather have. I don't know if they [her family] saw me as a threat or if they were afraid of my possibilities as a human being. Or maybe they were thinking I thought I was better than them, Anyway, I would say that they were somewhat stingy. Yes, they were stingy with their affection and attention toward me. And they were down right trifling in their behavior. But, they had a wealth, and sometimes, over abundance of criticisms! I just thank God for the positive influences in my life, like "DJ." I guess I should have started by saying (I hope he will not be upset with me), my name for "DJ" was not always "DJ." It was "Daddy D____." That's what I called him. I respect his wishes for me, now, not to use that name, because I can understand that. [She doesn't like me to use her first name either]. Now I refer to him as Daddy (I will probably always refer to him as that); or Dr. Dad, because I am so proud of him! He let nothing stop him from doing what he wanted to do; and when he gets tired, he's not afraid to let you know: "You know what? I'm tired!" Or as he fondly tells us, "You are giving me gas!" Not realizing that he gives us gas too! *But that's alright we love you anyway, Dad.* [There she goes throwing "love" into the situation. See what I mean?]

He is a very strong individual. It takes a strong person to not only be able to tell you something that's wrong, but also tell you something that's right and apologize for a misunderstanding. Or to simply say "I'm sorry," or "I'm not uncomfortable with that." I come from a family that wouldn't know what [that kind of] communication is, even if you directed them to it in Webster! Now, miscommunication? They're real good about. Not telling the whole truth? They are real, real good at that! Maybe that's why they are afraid? I have never been able to not speak my mind and not tell you the truth. I have felt love, strength and support in my relationship with my father. Perhaps one day… or maybe I'll do it now? Because I don't think my father has ever heard me sing. *Alright Dad, get ready for a "mushy" moment. I'm going to sing one verse and one chorus of a song. So you can never say you've never heard me sing before! It's easy because there's nobody here but God and me right now.* [And the voices of the children playing in the yard next door.] After listening to all of her recorded message, She begins to sing a song recorded by Celine Dione:

> *For all those times you stood by me,*
> *For all the truth that you made me see;*
> *For all the joy you brought to my life,*
> *For all the wrongs that you've made right;*
> *For all the dreams you made come true,*
> *For all the love I found in you,*
> *I'll be forever thankful, baby*
> *You're the one that held me up and never let me fall*
> *You're the one who saw me through, through it all*
>
> *You were my strength when I was weak,*
> *You were my voice when I couldn't speak,*
> *You were my eyes when I couldn't see,*
> *You saw the best there was in me.*
> *You picked me up when I couldn't reach*
> *You gave me faith cause you believed*
> *I'm everything I am because you loved me.*

She jokingly adds, *I really didn't need that help from the crow* [in the background]. *No background instruments or, you know, no background sounds are necessary here.* [As a musician, I was awe-struck! Her voice was clear, melodious and beautiful.]

Another important thing I learned from my father is to tell people how much you care...to show people how much you care, while they are here. *If I never say this to you again, I appreciate you. I adore you. I love you and I know you're always there when I need you. I just want you to know that I'm here when you need me! Now, enough of the mushy stuff. Let me get back to the story.*

As I said, Dad and I have known each other since Zion, and at some point he had problems and left. It's wonderful to have people who are trying to do the work of the Lord, but it's also, a wonderful thing to know that people are different: They think and behave differently, so sometimes in order to work together we have to put ourselves aside.

I can't say that very many people have been able to do that. Dad will always ask you, "What do YOU want to do?" Or "What do YOU THINK?" Half the time I don't know. She chuckles, BUT I'm glad he asks. *I'm glad you ask that question because it shows that you're not just thinking about what I want, but what the other person wants.* That is a significant part of the human being. Human beings care about human beings, at least they are supposed to care. I know he cares about me. I know he cares about his other children, his brother, even when we get on his nerves. He never stops showing and telling us that he loves us. He never stops trying to help us with whatever it is we are dealing with in our own lives. Sometimes, with the quick ones, he's able to work with us to help us figure out what we need; and the others ones, he just down right out tells you, "This is what you need to do!" Yes, my Dad has much attitude, if you haven't figured it out by now. But, that's why we love you, "FATHA!" [There she goes again.]

I have to say I really hated when he left Zion. I missed him terribly. I'm glad we've kept in touch all this time. I'm so glad he is in my life today. I thank him for introducing me to his extended family here in D.C.: Iisha, Willie and Sean. They are all beautiful people. Hopefully, God will bless others as he's blessed me in seeing the good in people. Seeing people that really care about you and they're not just faking. It's not just a facade. "DJ" has influenced a lot of people's lives and I'm glad to say he's been a special part of mine, and will continue to be so. I Love you, "FAVA!" (She laughs.) Now you know why.

Fifteen

June 1979. I was, and had been, struggling to find meaning and purpose in my life. I loved my parents dearly, but they did not take time out for me, or listen to me. At this time I did not have anyone to cling too or feel close to. Not my parents or my sister or any of my coaches. I say coaches because the only thing I was close to and very much in love with at that period in my life was the game of baseball.

I was real good at Baseball. I was a "left hander" who could play any position on the field and I have played them all. As a matter of fact, I was one of the first left-handed catchers (that anyone laid eyes on) who could really be a catcher. It was funny because people did not think that a left-handed person could be a catcher. You should have seen the people's faces as I "threw out" so many guys who were trying to steal bases. Once the other teams found out that I could throw players out, they stopped trying [testing] me. I also held pitching at heart. I used to pitch a lot of "no hitters" in major league. Not to brag on myself, but I was real special in this field. In fact, I was so good that I represented the city of Gary.

After all the festivities of opening day, my team, the defending champs, led the season off by [challenging] the runner-ups. I will never forget that day! This first game was [meant] to remind the other team that they would have to put in a lot of work if they were going to beat us. Our team took the field first and the crowd was ready to see the top contenders meet. As I was loosening up on the pitcher's mound, I was nervous because all those people and all the pretty little girls were watching, smiling and waving at me. [As] I prepared to pitch that game; I was so excited because I knew the parents [of my teammates] and a crowd would come out, especially the girls.

My parents didn't show up as usual. Don't get me wrong; they bought me new gloves, baseball spikes, jackets, sweatshirts and whatever I needed. I would have traded all those things in [even worn gym shoes and a raggedy glove, or played bare-handed] just to have seen my parents sitting in the bleachers cheering for me. Unfortunately, I had learned not to expect them at my games. But I was happy for everyone [else] who looked out there and saw his or her parents cheering for all of us. Some of [their] parents treated me as their own son and for that I was grateful.

I had pitched many games before, but this particular day was so exciting to me. I had my own little fan club with the players' mothers and a few girls that came just to see me, this [tall, slender] light skinned, brown-eyed kid. The umpire who yelled, "Let's play ball!" was my uncle (may he rest in peace). He had umpired senior or big league games, but never a major league game. That made this game even more special.

I could throw the ball fast, probably 70 to 75 M.P.H., which was fast in the majors. Everyone's mouth dropped when I pitched the first ball. Everything seemed to be moving in slow motion. I remember throwing that ball so fast that I fell down. As I looked up the ball had hit the batter right in the face. It happened so quickly that he did not even have time to move. Everyone was shocked, even me. People ran on to the field to tend to this guy, while my coach walked toward me to calm me down. He said, "Its okay, just settle down and pitch your game." The other player was all right but his face was swollen. He wanted to play so badly. I was relieved and at the same time I was pissed as I remember looking at him running toward first base smiling at me as though he was asking, "Is that all you got?" I struck the next three players out and won the game by pitching a "No hitter." I felt so good, I went home to celebrate, but my parents did not treat it as a special time for me. So, I just ate and went to bed feeling unloved and unwanted. All of those years I wanted my parents to be proud of me for being so gifted in something that I learned on my own, but as usual that never happened.

As my baseball career grew, the more I shut myself off from my family. I did not confide in anyone. As time moved on, the not confiding or getting someone to love me for me grew heavy on me. I found that I had another special little interest in making money for myself. I used to go around the neighborhood cutting grass and washing cars. I never knew or thought of meeting someone who I would later call my "Dad" and share much of my life with, i.e., my ups and downs, my all-around world. I never thought of getting close to anyone! I had locked myself into baseball and did not want anyone else in that world with me. I never imagined this beautiful man would help unlock my heart, so that I would be able to feel wanted. I wanted to be around this man constantly because of the love that he showed me, his ability to get on my level and understand. He was a shoulder to cry on and a hero to look up to. This man was D. Maurice Johnson. Excuse me, Dr. D. Maurice Johnson, my friend, my mentor, my hero, my dad.

The way we met was because he agreed to let me cut his grass one day. He was new in the neighborhood and I saw that his grass was real tall and needed cutting. So, I knocked on the door to ask if I could help him. He said, "Yes go ahead and cut it." He came out and held a conversation with me while I was working. He asked if I was from around here [the neighborhood] and what school I attended. They were simple questions and somehow I felt at ease with him. It was like some type of peace surrounded this guy. Now I realize that it was Jesus' love manifested through him. I told him my name was "Baby Boy." Check this out, he asked me for my real name! He has been calling me Leroy ever since. He said that I could regularly cut the grass and wash his car and his roommate Greg's car. I always went over there because Dad would spend time with me and listen to me and tell me that I was somebody. He used to always say, "Leroy, you are smart, intelligent, handsome and you have everything going for you, but it is up to you what you do with all those gifts."

He used to surprise me by showing up at some of my baseball games. I would all of a sudden look at the crowd and he was there. [It seemed that] out of nowhere he was there. Then, I'd look up again and he was gone. He used to come to my games and I never knew he had been there until afterward when I came over to his house. Then he would tell me that I [either] played a real good game or that I stunk. One thing about him, he did not mind telling you exactly how he felt or telling you the truth.

I grew up in the church, but all this guy did was stay in church! He was a choir director and most of his time was spent doing God's work. I got jealous at times because he did not spend enough time with me [due to his church obligations]. Being a kid, we don't always realize that adults have obligations that they must fulfill to survive. However, he did spend more time with me, then my own parents. So, I fell in love with this man instantly. He would hug me when I did good and verbally chastise me when I was not good. I'm grateful for that.

We built a good relationship between each other. My life was finally worth something to me. I always had my secret place when I was around Dad, where I could go and just be at peace. He adopted me as his son, not legally, but legally to him and me, and to God. I was his only son, and I was very proud to have him as my second father. Things were going well until he moved to Washington, D.C. It hurt me that he had to move. I started closing myself off again, but this time I took consolation in the streets. The streets had me – no doubt. And, no doubt, I knew his love for me would never end. He came looking for me whenever he was in Gary and spent some time with me. He gave me his number to call him at any time. But I did not call because of my activities in the street, i.e., the alcohol, drugs and women. My life now was about getting high and having sex. I no longer felt a purpose for my life. One day I called him and he told me that he wanted me to come stay with him. I think a parent knows just what their child needs, because I was so tired and lonely that his offer was just what I needed. So I moved to D.C. to get my life back on track. I was so happy to be with my Dad again! I knew if anyone could support me and put me back on track, Dr. Johnson could. After all he specializes in unconditional tender loving care.

I don't think Dad realized how far out there I really was. At first D.C. was very difficult for me because I had grown [quite accustomed] to a life in the streets. We argued a lot and he walked out on me, leaving me alone to think about what he had said. But he never, ever gave up on me. Many times he would put his life on hold to make sure that his baby (me) was on track doing something positive that would help me [grow and] prosper in life. He talked to me about putting my priorities together. I began to get myself together even though getting high was still a big part of my life. I started going to GED classes and working.

He still went to church doing the "choir director thing" and attending college at Howard University. Even though I only went to church with him once or twice, he used to always tell me how much God loved me and cared for me. He ministered to me with all of those "great" gospel songs. My favorite one was "Safe In His Arms." The Bible says, "Train a child in the way that he should go and when grown up he shall never depart from it". I've grown and now that song "Safe In His Arms" gives me the peace and love that Dad taught, or should I say instilled, in me. I just fell in love with those songs he played at home. I used to wait for him to leave, turn the volume on the sound system all the way up and dance all over the apartment to God's songs. All of this was bringing meaning back into my life.

Things were going well for us until I met this beautiful young lady. She was "fine" to me and I had to have her. Dad tried [to step in] to tell me to stay focused on what I had been doing, but this young lady just had my "nose wide open!" Once we started seeing each other, I started missing work, stopped trying or going to school and stopped studying for my G.E.D. just to be with her. I failed the G.E.D. test because I had been partying with this young lady all night and did not study. It did not matter because I was in love, or at least I thought that I was in love with this young lady.

When Dad got accepted in an internship program in New Orleans, he had to leave me once again. It crushed me that he was leaving but I knew how to hide myself during times of despair in my life. I acted like it was cool when *I was really tore down in the inside.* But, I was a man who had a girl so everything was going to be alright. *I never told you this until now.* When Dad left, I moved in with one of dad's closest friends, Robert or "Chattie" who let me stay with him for about a week. I fondly called him "Uncle Robert" because he meant so much to me, May He Rest In Peace. Times got really hard for me when I went back to Gary. I was trying to keep my girl and myself together. Again, I went back to the streets.

To sum this all up, I am now in prison doing 15 years for those streets. Guess what? Dad is still with me even through all of this. That, in itself, should tell you something about him. He's been so much of a hero to me. I've always perceived a hero to be superhuman. Well, to me, this brother is a superhuman who has the power of God all in him. [Thanks, son.] The Bible says, "How precious are the feet of those who preach the gospel." Dr. Johnson's feet are very precious to me and my siblings, his godchildren; as well as all those who come in contact with him. A special man, a fervent man, a "God" man. He's been a knight in shining armor to me, one who through all things has never given up on me. And now, I've been called to preach the good news of Jesus Christ! This brother has been that wheel inside of a wheel for me, always encouraging, understanding and lifting me up. Crying with me, laughing with me, praying with me and teaching me to be an effective person in society. My dad is the greatest on this Earth to me. Thank you, Dad for loving me, taking me up under your wing and showing me that Jesus is so real, because I've seen him inside of you.

God Bless you Dad,
Your son,

Leroy

P.S. – I hope you can read this…a lot of misspelled words. Check it carefully, done in a rush.

Sixteen

My name is Iisha and I am the youngest of - Maurice's, excuse me, D. Maurice Johnson's - godchildren. I first met my dad, if I'm not mistaken, when I was a sophomore in high school. I was attending Gethsemane Baptist Church at the time. I walked in church one day and I noticed we had a new musician on the organ. I asked around about him and they said, "He's our new Minister of Music for the church and he'll probably be in charge of the youth choir."

I was real shy at the time and I didn't know how to perceive him because there were plenty of people in the church that I didn't talk to just because I didn't trust them. But after a couple of Sundays, I went up to Dr. Johnson and I introduced myself. I told him who I was, what I sang and things like that. He seemed like a really cool guy. When I first met him, he instantly started cracking jokes and stuff. He really made me feel at ease.

As time progressed, I noticed that I could tell him anything. I think…it didn't even take a month or two before I started telling Dr. Johnson about myself as far as what school I went to, who my parents were, what types of things I liked to do for fun and in that nature. But, he always knew that I was only talking above the surface. He always knew that there was something else going on inside of me deep within. He would always ask me what was wrong or if there was anything that he could do. [He told me] that he would always be there to help me no matter what. It took some time, but I remember I'd had a falling out with my mom, like I always did. This time I just couldn't hold it in. I remember [that] Sunday after service I rushed right into Dr. Johnson's office, and closed the door and said, "I need to talk to you – it's important." He could see that I was very upset, so, he locked the door, told everyone else to go away, and we sat there and talked. By the end of our conversation, a half-hour later, I felt so good about myself. I was so pleased. I felt like a big weight had just been lifted off my head. From that time on I realized that I could tell Dr. Johnson anything. And that he was not there to judge me, he was not there to criticize me, he was there to listen and to help make things better.

As the months moved on, we started getting closer. I would call him at home if it was important. If things were just getting unbearable at home, I would just call him at [his] home. Or I would go to a friend's house to call him and we would just talk. I really felt like he really understood me and what I was going through. I had never had a friend like Dr. Johnson before in my life. I truly felt like he was my best friend. He never let me down no matter what. Yes, there were times when he couldn't talk to me, but he would always try to call me as soon as he had some free time. At times I really didn't understand why he wouldn't call me back right away, but then I also realized that he had a lot of other priorities besides me and a lot of times [other] things were going to have to come before me. I guess you could say six months into or friendship/relationship, he started calling me his "little Princess." I have to admit, he had little nicknames and jokes for everybody else in the choir, but when he called me his little Princess, it would make my face just light up when I heard that. When he would call me his little Princess I would start calling him Dad. It was just so amazing because I felt like I had a special place in his heart. A special place that no one else could take away from me, that no one else could be a part of. It was just me! And, no matter what, he would never go anywhere. Well, that's not always true...so I learned. Everything is not always a *bed of roses*, as you might call it.

I guess it was a year and a half (or two years) after we had known each other he left Gethsemane. That shattered my world! I was so used to coming in every Sunday morning and seeing him sitting on the organ, or sitting on the piano, or hearing his loud obnoxious voice in the choir room. I just felt like he was leaving me [and] he was betraying me. I felt like once he left he was going to forget all about me, we weren't going to be friends anymore, he wasn't going to be there for me, [and] I wouldn't have anybody to talk to. All those things were running in my head. I even went to talk with him about it. He told me, "Iisha, that's not going to happen. Whenever you need me just call me and I'll be there for you."

In the past, people have always told me they would be there for me. Even if they were moving away or leaving or something like that. They always said, "Oh, Iisha I'll be there for you. All those people let me down, but not my dad. I would call him sometimes and we would have conversations for an hour or an hour and a half. It was just so amazing. I felt closer to him [since he had left] the church than I felt at any other given time. At that point, I really didn't realize that my dad really, truly and undeniably loved me - no matter what.

To be truthful and honest with you, I treated him as my parent. I didn't get to see him much, at all. There was rarely a time when I did get to see him. Whenever my report card came I always mailed it to him with a letter. Even before I would mail them, I would always tell him, "Hey Dad, I didn't do so good in this, but I promise I'll bring it up next quarter," or "Dad, I had a little trouble in this, but it will be Ok next quarter." He would never get upset or anything. He would just always say, "Iisha, just tell me before I see it for myself. Let's talk about this: What happened in this area? How can you improve yourself?" My dad never once tore me down. He never once tried to belittle me at all. That's one thing that I have to say that I love about my dad. I know with my mom and my stepfather, there were times where [I felt] I just couldn't do anything right. Either I was always getting yelled at, on punishment, couldn't go anywhere, [and] couldn't talk on the telephone. I mean, there were times when Iisha was just a major screw up in the family. [Not so, Baby!] But with my dad I never screwed up! I could come home with a "C" and although he really didn't like it, he accepted it [because he] knew that I was doing my best. With my mom, my butt would stay in the house. I was automatically grounded. You know, my dad said that he didn't really like [agree with] the methods that my mom was using with me, but he couldn't say anything about them for the simple fact that I was not living with him. I must say, even though I was grounded my dad always made me feel good about my grades.

On every birthday my dad would call. He would send me a card. During Christmastime, he might not have had a lot of money, but he would always do something special that would just (he doesn't know) fill my heart completely. I remember one year in particular, December 1996. My dad had told me, right around Thanksgiving, that he really didn't have any money to buy me a Christmas present, but he was still going to give me something. When Christmastime came I went to his house to get my Christmas present. It was a [audiocassette] tape. At first I was like, OK...He's really being cheap. I can't believe this. When he told me that he couldn't give me a present, I'll admit – I thought "Hey, maybe he's joking." Maybe he's going to give me this or he's going to give me that or he's going to give me some money or something. But, no...he really did just give me a tape. I was like, "Oh, this is pure-T - B.S. I went home and listened to it. I don't even think my dad even knew this: a lot of the songs I loved. A couple of them were like my favorite songs. For like two months after I got that tape, I would listen to that tape at night and I would fall asleep to it. I'm pretty sure my dad doesn't know that. [You're right.]

May 30, 1995. I was finally walking across that stage to get my diploma. My dad and I had been talking off and on. I was real busy with school and work, and he was real busy teaching, going to school and things of that nature. We really didn't have that much contact with each other. So, I sent him an invitation to my graduation. He told me, "Iisha, I'm gonna be there." I remember as I walked down the aisle on my graduation day, I looked up and saw my dad standing there. It just brought tears to my eyes. [I cried for a long time after the ceremony had started.] I was just so happy. Yeah, I know my mom, grandmother and people that I loved were there, but it just filled my heart to know that my dad was there. He was looking and watching his youngest daughter graduate! It just meant so, so much to me. After the ceremony dad walked up to me and kissed me. He told me, "Baby, I am so proud of you. I'm so proud of you and I love you. I hope you didn't think I was going to miss this day. I cleared my schedule so I could spend the entire day with you." We left there and went to my house for my graduation party. All the people who loved me and wanted to be with me were there. I had family and friends there, but most importantly, I had my dad there. That was really all that mattered. It seemed like there was a standstill when he walked in – all I could see was my dad. It felt so incredibly special to me.

In the fall of that same year I went to Elon College. That was one of the most [difficult] things that I had to do because I had to leave my dad. We had been in the same state for about five years. Even though I was only going five hours away, it was a [struggle] because I wasn't used to being [so far] away from my dad. I knew that if I really wanted to [talk with him] he was only an exit away from me, [but that will not be possible from North Carolina.] The first night I got to school, I called my dad to tell him how much I missed him. He told me that I could call him collect, but only once per week. [He reassured me] that I was going to be OK and that he was (and always would be) with me in spirit. If I ever needed anything all I had to do was call him.

I remember a specific time during my freshman year when I was extremely broke. I wasn't in the habit of asking my dad for any type of money - no matter what. But, this time I did because I had no other choice. I understood when he told me that he really did not have it. I think that really shocked him because I guess he expected me to be upset or to be mad. But I wasn't. He immediately asked me to find out where the closest Western Union was located and to call him back. When I called back he told me some money would be there within the hour. Once again, the tears started flowing. [We call that sniffling and snotting.] My dad always knows how to make a person sniffle and snot. I didn't know what to do. There was so much joy when my best friend took me to Western Union to pick up the $80.00 that he had sent me. I was just so happy that I did not know what in the world to do. My dad had just made my day. I called him to say thank you and I love you. He just didn't know how much that meant to me. He said, "OK, you're giving me gas. Get off my phone!" My freshman year wasn't really that bad. I would call my dad to tell him the new experiences that I was getting into. He said, "Yeah, it's about time you experienced that because you are in school [college] now and those types of things happen. Just be careful and take care of yourself. Don't let anybody use you." My dad always had advice for me.

When I came home on breaks I tried to spend every waking moment with my Dad. [He would plan things for us to do, but remind me that he still had other professional commitments to honor.] He said, "I will try to spend as much time as I can with you, just remember, my time doesn't stop because you come home." During the summer after my freshman year I worked at Enterprise Children's Center. It was inevitable that I would see my dad once a week, I had to see him. It was getting really bad. I couldn't go two days without talking to him [and checking up on him.] As he calls me, I was his "mother hen" at times. I am the youngest child, but I always played [assumed] the role of being his mother. I worried about him. Even when he was not home, I would leave messages on his answering machine asking him if he was doing what he needed to do to be healthy. He told me I was so worrisome. I wanted a full report on his well being even down to the results of his checkups. [Mind you, I had to pull teeth to get that same information about her.] Those were the [same]questions he would have to ask me, but he never did.

It was time to return to Elon for my sophomore year. It was an emotional experience for me because I was thinking about pledging a sorority. I had already told my dad and he knew that I wanted to do this all my life. But, my mom told me that I needed to wait until my junior year. I felt like I was ready to pledge emotionally, spiritually, physically and mentally. Well, God had other plans in store for me. When I first started pledging I was a complete and utter wreck! I would call my dad, Lord have mercy, every night begging him to come visit me. I just needed my dad to come visit me. I just needed him there. I'm sure other kids or young people reading this [have realized] there are times when you just need your parent. When that happens, there's no wait, no stop, there's no anything. It's just - I need you. You've got to come now. He kept telling me that he could not leave right now, but "lo and behold," my dad left Maryland to come see me. (That made me feel so good.) He only came for the weekend, but that time we spent together just made my entire fall semester! I'm here to tell you that just by him coming that weekend it really helped me finish the pledging process. December 1, 1997, I "crossed the burning sands" and became a full-fledged member. I told my dad that I would never forget what he did for me. He really did enable me and give me the strength to finish the goal I had set for myself.

When I returned home for Christmas and winter break, my dad hit me with a bomb. I guess it was around February or March. He told me he was getting married. I don't know if you remember the first shatter to my world: he left Gethsemane. The second shatter to my world was when he told me that he was getting married. First of all, I didn't like the woman at all. Second of all, I felt like she was going to come between our relationship. That's what I was afraid of. To tell you the truth: I tried everything I could to break them up. I basically, told my dad how I felt until there was nothing else I could do. I'll never forget the day my dad got married. I didn't like it, but I was one of her bridesmaids and I did stand up there. I told my dad before the wedding even started, "If this is something you really want to do I will stand by you. But if it's not, we can walk out of this church right now, the car is still running!" My dad said, "No, Baby, I got this, I want to do this." I said, "OK."

My dad and I have been through so, much together. One of my really vivid memories of how he really came through for me was when I dropped out of college in December 1997. I didn't think there was anything else that I could do or anyone that I could turn to. When I came home, my mom and I was not getting along. She had decided that it was best if I moved out. At the time all I had was a temporary job. There was no way I could just move out on [the income from] a temporary job, but my mom thought it was best that I leave. So, I did the only thing I could do – I went to daddy for help.

I'll never forget, a couple of days after my birthday (March 10,1998), I showed my dad the place I found at Fountain Club Apartments in New Carrollton and he liked it. He was reluctant about leasing the apartment in his name because he could not afford the rent if something were to happen to me. [Plus, I was still paying for debts I incurred trying to help other people! I could not afford to be burned again.] But, on March 14, we signed a one-year lease [for my first apartment.] Once again, my dad had come through for me with flying colors! My dad never left me out there. There were times when he would tell me I should not have done this or that, but when there came a time that I needed my dad the most, he was always there – no matter what. Regardless if he wanted to deal with it or not. After I got my apartment, it seemed that my dad and I just got closer. We always saw each other; everyday or every other day. If we didn't see each other we were on the phone, it didn't make a difference if it was one, two or three hours. We found things to talk about. I love to talk and my dad is the same exact way.

My dad kept telling me that I needed to go back to school and get a degree because I would not make it in this world without one. I would be like, "Yeah, yeah, yeah." I was a normal young adult who was so happy about making a little bit of money that I didn't care about going back to school. I really didn't. That was the least of my priorities at the time. I will tell you that in February 1999, I enrolled in George Washington

University with the help of my job. They had a tuition reimbursement plan where you put up the money and they paid you back after finishing the classes. Fortunately, I didn't have to go that route. When I explained to them what was happening, they paid my tuition [at the onset] so that I could get a better position. It took a lot out of me. I worked from 7:00 AM – 12:00 PM; then attended school from 1:00 – 9:00 or 10:00 at night. I was burning it at both ends from February to December, but I didn't care, I was determined to get my degree! The real blessing was that I had completed all the core credits while at Elon. So, I only needed six classes to graduate when I changed my major to journalism, which is my current profession. Thank you, Lord. In December 1999, I was conferred with a Bachelors of Art degree in Journalism.

Dad, I know you are probably doing your dance or about to do your dance. [I sure am!] I was so excited and happy to have been able to accomplish that, and furthermore, to make my dad proud of me. Nobody could take my joy away. Right after I graduated, I decide it was time to get a car. My dad had been telling me that I needed one for two years. After a while I got tired of hearing that. [And she nearly got stranded in Reston, Virginia one night!] December 30, 1999 at around 1:00 PM, I walked into Capitol Toyota and at 7:00 PM I walked out, excuse me; I drove off the lot in a brand new, 4-door 1997 Toyota Corolla. My dad was so incredibly proud of me, that he danced all over his house a couple of times. Once again, I made my dad proud of me. [Sure did!]

Now, in my opinion, there are only a couple of other triumphs that I have to make in life: to get my masters degree, get married, and make my daddy a grandfather. [Sniffle, sniffle, snot.] I know those things will come in time, but the one thing that I have to say is, "Daddy, I love you with all my heart and with all my soul. Believe me…I would not be the woman that I am today without you. We've known each other for ten years and I have grown to become the most beautiful, most educated and most knowledgeable woman that you see before you today. [You forgot modest.] I owe all that to you and my other father, Jesus Christ. You were there: when I needed you, when I needed an ear, when I wanted to talk my head off about anything – you were there! You never gave up on me. You never let me down. There may have been times when I didn't get what I wanted, but you were there for me. I love you for that.

Daddy, You just don't realize that you are the best dad that a girl could ever wish or hope or ask for. I hope you are "sniffling and snotting" right now because I'm really about to start. I just wanted to let you know that I could not be where I am today without you and I just want you to remember that. You have to thank yourself and I have to thank God over and over again. Every night before I go to bed, I always thank him for letting you be a part of my life. If it had been up to others, you would not have been a part of my life. God only knows where I would have been then. Dad, I am the woman that you see today because of you. I'll never forget you, no matter what, daddy. I love you and God Bless you."

[Whew! How is one man supposed to endure all those kind words without "sniffling and snotting?" You are who you are today because you worked hard at it! I love you too.]

Seventeen

In the beginning everything [in my life] was hazy. Nothing was clear or concrete. Then one day the haze started fading away. I met "DJ" in my senior year of high school. I had no plans or sense of direction. Nor did I have a home. I mean, I wasn't completely on the street, but I wasn't far from it either. Through a mutual friend we "hooked up" and he allowed me to move in with him as a temporary place to stay until I completed high school. To my surprise, all the components [that I had been] missing [in my life] were found at his address. Neither one of us ever stopped to think that we would have such an impact on each other's life.

At first I was very skeptical. I mean, to take a street kid out of the ghetto and move him to the suburbs, was just asking for trouble. I remember I couldn't sleep well because of the eerie silence. Not to mention, I did not trust or believe in anyone because on the streets nothing's free. That was the mentality that I was carrying with me. I was the type of person who had what I now call the "OWOTS" or own way of thinking syndrome. And most often people who live life with this perception are destined for trouble. However, I did have a good heart, but because of the lack of love in my life I had a terrible time displaying one of my best character traits. "DJ" somehow managed to maneuver his way through that tangled web that led to my heart. That's when the learning process started.

While in high school I was interested in music and at the time, I didn't know that "DJ" was a Registered Music Therapist. I was definitely in need of therapy, so that was the level that we first connected on. Plus, the fact that he was a substitute teacher at the high school that I attended. I felt so alone and hurt. [It seemed] as if no one cared if I breathed the same air that they did or occupied the same space that they did. So I had this "F_ _ _" the world attitude. Also, I intended to hurt, or get even with, every living soul that ever caused me hurt or pain. Sharing this allows me to keep growing and learning. That's the process of life. *Thanks, "DJ."*

"DJ" and I had our first confrontation one morning on the way to school, just before classes started. I never had a male figure before "DJ" to give me a sense of security regarding who I am. I don't particularly remember exactly what the argument was, however, I told him that he had to be a father all the time, not just when I'm making good decisions, but when I make the "not so good ones" as well. He told me that he felt odd disciplining a child that was not his own.

"DJ" taught me about interacting as a young adult with older adults. He showed me that older adults have a different more "settled" approach on life. Also, they are more determined to achieve on a higher level where as younger adults are more prone to want to be a part of the clubbing scene, the movies, or just out having a good time, myself included. Now however, I'm more focused on the challenges that may lie ahead of me and whether or not I'm on the right path. I often feel like I'm lacking in more areas [than] I would like to, or should be, at this time, but "DJ" is always there with positive input and a deeper perspective for me to try. I believe I have unique qualities and skills that would be very beneficial in whatever I choose to do, however, I keep getting stumped when trying to apply those attributes consistently on a daily basis. I mean, there's so many things I enjoy doing, that I don't want to let any of it go long enough to develop interests that would allow me to be financially equipped to expand my horizons to my next level of livelihood and other experiences. I have known "DJ" now for seven years. Some people would say that seven is a charmed number. I don't know if that's true, but let's wait and see. If that is so, you'll be reading another book. Now wouldn't that be great!

Now, on to the more serious matters. It's been a really wonderful time in my life. The experiences were worth the time it took to live them. It was through "DJ" that I met my God-sister, Iisha. She's a character all by herself, and then some. [True dat!] I remember once I went on a road trip with some friends to North Carolina and I ended up getting stranded. Well, needless to say, my little sister offered to help. She was attending Elon College at the time. When I finally got there she introduced me to her roommate and some of her friends. A few days into my stay we got into an argument and she kicked me out. That's right! We'd just had one of the biggest snowstorms in recent years. And wouldn't you know that I would be the one to get thrown into that storm. [Monique's response: Hilarious story – sounds just like something Iisha would do.]

Now, I'm in this little small college town just outside of Burlington, North Carolina. I must have looked like some juvenile delinquent [or thug] because that's what the police officer that pulled me over said. He asked had I ran away from the detention center! I began to explain the situation that had just occurred between my God-sister and me. As we drove to the police station, he was telling me about some daily labor jobs that I could work to make the amount of money it would cost me to get home. Someone suggested that we call Iisha, so we did. She acted as if she didn't know I existed. As if things could get any worst! The thought of me having to stay in a shelter until then was completely exhausting. Eventually, I was on my way to the shelter via police escort. [Monique's response: sorry Willie. Food for thought: Always have your own transportation].

When I finally got to the shelter, there were homeless people lined outside in front of the building waiting to get in. I was shocked at how many families I saw. I did whatever they asked me to do and assisted in any way that I could. I helped set the table for the food. We said a prayer, then sat down and ate. The meal itself was good: soup, crackers, fruit drink and fruit cocktail. So, out of that unfortunate turn of events, my heart was blasted [hurting] by what was going on outside of me and in the rest of my world.

I called everyone that I could think of to try to come up with the money to go home. No one would help me and that's when I figured that there was no one for me to turn to. Frustrated, I begin to walk. I ended up borrowing a pick-up truck from a nameless friend. I also had to borrow the gas. Thankfully, I made it home. Since then, Iisha and I have been able to piece together a nice wholesome relationship, which makes "DJ" very happy! She still "irks" me from time to time, but over all our relationship is wonderful. That's the way it should be with siblings.

"DJ" has been a good role model for me and has had a significant impact on my life. A true father and friend. I'm blessed each day that I wake up knowing I'm loved and cared for daily. It is important for males to have someone [an adult male] that they can look to for guidance and support. Thanks "DJ" for allowing me the opportunity to give back some of what you have given to me. You are truly a special person to me.

Thank You,
Willie

[You're welcome, son.]

Eighteen

July 1, 2000

Hello D___.,

> *This is such a beautiful gesture and expression of love. I know Chris would be pleased and happy. Her "cheeks would be hitting the ceiling" as she described her happiness when she smiled. I, too, am very pleased. Chris often spoke of you with kindness and appreciation. I'm glad Chris was able to share so much with you. She admired you, as did others, but you were a good friend and mentor to her. She and I appreciated you being there more than you'll ever know. Thank you for your thoughtfulness.*

> *Your sister in Christ,*

> *Seri E. Nolan*

That was an excerpt of a letter from Christina's mother, a posthumous contribution from Chris. I am not sure how she felt about her relationship with me or whether she considered me a father figure or not, but I certainly considered her to be like a daughter to me.

This was the last letter that I received from David:

July 27, 1990
1:00 p.m.

Dear D____.,

    What's going on, podner [partner], How are you doing? Fine, I hope. Well, I really don't know where to start. I am just so happy and proud of myself. First of all, I just wanted to tell you thanks for everything, man. You're the best friend a man could ever have. You're just like a Dad to me. I look up to you and I love you man!!!!! (Smile) Let me tell you something...I knew I had it in me every since I was in pre-school because I was very intelligent and very smart. (Ha! Ha!) Of course you always knew that, right? Of course! Because you were for sure and had a positive attitude that I was going to make it. But let me tell you how the story goes.

    For a minute I was nervous, I thought I wasn't going to graduate. I was real scared and didn't know what to do. It felt like my whole life was going to be over because I noticed during my last semester you weren't really with me at all! [I'm sorry.] But like I said, I guess you knew that I was going to make it, <u>and I did.</u> I was so happy and didn't know what to do when I walked across the stage seeing all my family and friend's smiling faces. It just made me feel like <u>I was it</u>. And I knew it! I wish you could have been there to see your son, man. [Me too!] Oh, by the way, I'm sorry that I didn't get to make it to your graduation either. I guess that's why you didn't come to mine, huh? But <u>God still loves us</u>, dude. (Smile) [No. I would not have been that petty with you.]

105

Well, enough about that. Let me tell you about this desert [Arizona] and the mountains, dude. It's really hot up here and very dry. That heat doesn't be playing up here, it is serious, man. The city is real nice and clean here, nice houses, nice jobs, very nice looking young and old women. (Ha! Ha!) But that's not what I am up here for. [Yeah, right!] I am here for school at the Phoenix Institute of Technology (PIT). My teacher, Mr. Kilburn is real nice and very funny. He looks exactly like Tom Landry who used to coach the cowboys. PIT is a big school and I know my way around it already. I have some good news to tell you...my classroom average is 90. Yes! Man, I am really shocking myself. I didn't know I was really this smart until I got away from my family and friends. The class I am taking is ELECTRONICS! Sorry the letters are so big, but I am just so happy because I am about to make it.

One more thing, in your letter you said something about the Nation's Capitol. Let me tell you a big secret...in two years I'll be owning the Capitol. (Ha! Ha! Ha!) Well, I'm about to go. I have to go to a job interview at Embassy Suites hotel. I hope I get it. Wish me luck. I want you to always remember I LOVE YOU!!!!!!!!!! May God bless us both. I miss you. Be cool.

Yours truly, your son,

David

*****

In the short time that we were allowed to share with each other, Christina and David, each of them in their own way allowed me the privilege of being like a father figure to them. They may not be in the land of the living, but memories of them are alive in my heart. I loved them! They were so full of promise, potential, and possibilities. They greatly inspired me in different ways as together we struggled to become more faithful disciples of Jesus Christ and better human beings. I will forever cherish our relationships. "God rest their precious souls."

YET YOU LIVE

Two lights from my life are gone,
Two voices I loved to hear are stilled
There are two vacant places in my heart
Which I know can never again be filled
I may not have their presence anymore
But I will cherish their love in my heart
forevermore.

With all my love,

DJ

"…Blessed are the dead which die in the Lord from henceforth: Yea, saith the Spirit,
that they may rest from their labours and their works do follow them."
Revelation 14:13

D. Maurice Johnson

"...So now also Christ shall be magnified in my body whether it be by life, or by death. For me to live is Christ, and to die is gain."
Philippians 1:20b - 21

Nineteen

Daniel Jr. or "DJ" is six years old, soon to be seven. He is the firstborn child of Daniel Sr. and Rená. We share the same nickname of "DJ." From the time he was born, I have referred to him as my "namesake." He blushes each time I greet with a hug and say, "Hi, my namesake." He would respond, "Hi, my namesake." We now refer to him as "little DJ" to distinguish between the two of us. I also find myself calling him Daniel Jr. more because he is getting older and more sensitive about who he is.

"Little DJ" loves music! At his age he beats time very well on the drums, which he loves very much. Every time he comes to my house he wants to play on the drums. When there are no drums present he finds a pencil or some other objects to serve as his drum and drumsticks. I recently received a note from his mother that said: "DJ told me to remind you about the drumsticks that you said you would get him for his birthday. And no – he does not forget anything." He gets equally excited about the piano. He likes to experiment with the sounds and push the keys to accompany the music that is going on in his head. "Little DJ" is bold about his singing. If you strike up a tune he knows he will sing along with you. He has been known to strike up a tune that we have been rehearsing without any warning. Many times we thought he was not even paying attention to what we were singing. I have been told that he stands in the aisle imitating me while I am conducting the choir.

"Little DJ" is a complex person. He is bright, funny, energetic, creative, and inquisitive. He observes his environment and notices even the slightest change. He asks the questions that most people only wonder about – and, he expects an answer. [*Rená remarks, "Yes, He does."*] "Little DJ" is quick to flash a great big smile while holding a conversation with him. He is decisive, in that, he knows what he wants and likes. Most times he persists until he gets what he wants. You may be able to distract him for a moment with his favorite foods: macaroni and cheese, and eggs. He remembers everything that he hears and typically reminds us of that at times that are awkward for us. He has a gift for asking questions or making statements that leave us with our mouths hanging wide open or laughing so hard that it hurts. I suspect "Little DJ" will probably become a performer and a people-oriented person.

Now, DeAndre is quite a different story. The very first time I saw him, I looked into his pretty little green eyes saying "Hey Man," and he immediately flashed one of the biggest smiles that I have ever seen on a baby. Ever since that time he has become my baby! He was such a cute little baby boy.

DeAndre is five years old and the second child of Daniel Sr. and Rená. We have had so many nicknames for him. As a infant he was called "Yay-Yay" because his brother could not say baby; and as a toddler he was "yay." His little face used to light up every time he would see me, hug me, or hear me call him "Hi, my namesake," just like I called his brother. Sometimes he still refers to me as "namesake." But today, we call him "Dre" now that he is in school.

It is so fascinating to watch as DeAndre begins to develop his own personality. For the most part, he was a very jolly baby. Always smiling, cooing, and willing to let you hold him. But when DeAndre is in one of his moods all he wants is his mother. [*Rena remarks, "So true."*] At times when he is tired, sleepy, sick, hungry or waking up, he will not smile or talk or let you hold him. He just wants to be left **A-L-O-N-E**! He is a strong-willed boy who will steadfastly hold out for what he wants. He will not budge until he is ready to shift. You will immediately know if he likes you by whether or not he responds to you. If he is feeling moody he may not respond to those of us he likes! And if you do not leave him alone, <u>he will</u> fuss you out! Sometimes he allows us to bribe him using his favorite foods: mashed potatoes and string beans. [*Rená remarks, "and don't forget CANDY!"*]

DeAndre strikes me as a leader and a trendsetter. He thinks fast on his feet and has an uncanny skill of employing appropriate but witty responses. He is gradually becoming one who creates rather than one who copies. One thing that we will definitely have to contend with is his temperamental nature. I suspect he has been gifted with artistic creativity but I have not validated my suspicions as of yet. My instincts tell me that eventually he will use his honesty and natural charm to change lives and situations in positive ways.

Alphonso Jr. or "AJ" is five years old. He is the firstborn child of Alphonso Sr. and Nee Nee. When he was a baby he would only respond to other people in the presence of his parents. He would cry the minute his parents were out of his sight, even if they were just in the next room. There were times when I had to keep "AJ" because his parents had to take care of business matters. I used to walk him from room to room in my house, talking with him, and letting him touch different objects in the rooms. If that did not work we would look out the window. For some reason that always worked. It was then that I realized "AJ" had an inquisitive nature. He liked to explore things to see how they worked.

As "AJ" got older he gradually began to feel comfortable enough around me that he would not cry as easily. But his parents still had to be around. It took less time to stop him from crying. I guess he was getting used to the routine I used to calm him down. I felt so good the very first time he came to church with his dad, who is a percussionist. When he saw me he broke out running toward me saying, "Hi, "DJ." I was so surprised that I picked him up and kissed him in the top of his head as I returned his greeting. From then on he had me hooked. I tried to give him all the candy that I kept in my briefcase for the children at church. Once he got some candy he would go back to sit with his father. After that, he never settled down in church until he spoke to me and got his candy. Eventually he got to the place where he would sit with me during the service. I was beginning to notice "AJ" felt more at ease when the routines were predictable.

The other thing I observed was that "AJ" was a very charming little boy. The members of the church loved him! He allowed them to spoil him rotten. They would hug and kiss him and he would sit with them. Some of them even gave him money. By the same token "AJ" was learning that he could escape boundaries and limits by flashing that charming smile or easing toward his father. What he also had to realize was "DJ" don't play that! Several times I spoke to him about correcting his behavior and he ran to his father so I let him off the hook. But one day he was acting out so much that I gave him the "evil" eye. He tried to ignore me, but I grabbed him before he could make his escape. He was so surprised by my actions that he began to cry. His dad, who had been watching the whole thing, supported me. He laughed and said, "Uh-huh, You'd better listen to "DJ" because he'll get your butt if you don't mind him. And you had better listen to him when he speaks to you!" Today, "AJ" knows I will correct him regardless to who is around or where we are. The corrective incidents are far less though.

"AJ" loves McDonald's chicken nuggets, hamburgers, collard greens and fried chicken. His mom says, "He can tear up some fried chicken!" His father and I know that he gets that honestly because we both share the same feeling about fried chicken. Another thing that "AJ" loves is music. He gets excited when the music begins to play. It is not uncommon to see him beating on the drums while his father is playing or trying to play the piano while he is sitting on the bench with me. I have been told that he stands in the aisle – in church - imitating me while I am conducting the choir. I think the curious side of "AJ" is causing him to become bolder about trying new things, even if he tries them reluctantly. I envision him as a brilliant scientist and a performer of some kind.

Brianna is four years old and the second child of Alphonso Sr. and Nee Nee. Her little face lights up every time I call out, "Bri-Bri" or "My Angel Girl." For the longest time she would never respond to me at all. She never allowed me to touch her or hold her. The only thing she would do is look at me like I was an alien. Her parents say she treated everyone like that. I had hoped that she would become more comfortable around me after I used my calming routine on her. Wrong! She withdrew even more. We only connected after her parents repeatedly encouraged her to interact with me, and when she saw how well "AJ" related to me.

I am still trying to figure Brianna out. She is a very cautious little girl when it comes to relating to other people. She is temperamental, in that, when she opens up to you it may be only for a fleeting moment on that day. She may not even allow you to come near her the next time you see her. If she does not want to be bothered she will cling to her mother. Sometimes she does not even respond to her own father! Plus, she will quickly fuss at you or whack you when she is displeased.

When it comes to food she eats everything, but she likes pasta and pizza. You do not want to be around her when she is hungry or thirsty. At those times she becomes very evil especially if she has to wait. She really loves her brother. On one hand, they fight like cats and dogs all the time. He knocks her down, runs her over and aggravates her to no end. For some reason she tolerates all the things he does to her. But when Brianna reaches her limit she simply slaps his face to make him stop. On the other hand, if you mess with "AJ" she attacks you with all that is within her, even if she has just finished smacking him. I have seen her try to defend "AJ" from her parents and from me. The other thing she does is comforts him when he has been punished. It is so adorable to watch her rub his back or pat him when he is crying. Her stance is clear, "No one bothers my brother except me. Anyone who does will have to deal with me!"

Brianna is beginning to develop her own personality. She is possessive of her things and protective of people who are dear to her. Brianna has a natural gift for humor. She is really quite funny even when she does not mean to be. She makes us laugh with the facial expression that she makes when we ask her questions. She looks so confused and her voice rises when she asks, "Huh?" Her response gives the impression that she is so confused or either you are stupid for asking her such a question. Other times, she responds in a way that catches you completely off guard because it is so funny. Then she looks at us like we are crazy because she did not mean for it to be funny. When she realizes that it was funny, she laughs too. Brianna seems to have natural leadership ability. She knows what she wants and puts forth the effort to get it. She also knows how to be flexible enough to get what she wants. I suspect that she will probably be a politician or legislator because of her forceful and persuasive nature and her tendency to advocate for the well being of others.

Overall, both sets of parents have encouraged interaction between us and reinforced my role in the lives of their children in private and in public. I am grateful that they have sanctioned and endorsed our special relationship. Oh, how I anticipate the day when all of them can share their own perspective of their relationship with me.

While serving as the Minister of Music & Arts at Church of the Redeemer (UMC), playing for the youth choir was a part of my responsibilities. It was from this experience that I met two very fine gentleman, Charles and Yeolman. From first impression you would think they were meek and mild mannered individuals. But if you had the opportunity to spend any time with them alone you would soon discover that they were quite the opposite.

At the time Yeolman and I met, he was a seventeen-year old senior in high school. He kept to himself most of the time. He would never say very much in a group, but we have had several profound discussions in private. He always seems so serious. I later found out that he was a very troubled young man looking to find the silver lining in a cloud. One day, he approached me and asked me if I would be his dad. I was honored and before I could really think about it I said "yes."

Since that time, I have had the opportunity to spend some quality time with him. Many times I would return home to find him sitting in front of my house driving a car that I did not recognize. I think he knows that I have had several conversations with his mother who has recently had to raise him as a single parent. What I have found out is that he is an extremely sensitive young man with a big heart, strong wit, and uncanny sense of humor. I also learned he is the king of diversionary tactics. He knows how to avoid things very tactfully and very quickly. [His mother concurs.]

When Charles and I met he too was a seventeen-year old senior in high school. He was the life of the party, a clown. He took great pride in being able to entertain others. I would get so disturbed by his subtle antics during rehearsals. He knew I was upset whenever I called his whole name out in public. He hated that! At other playful times, I used to just walk up to him and palm the back of his nice round head for no reason. He hated that too!

We bonded because Charles was also a musician. He was in the school marching band, and several other choirs, so he was always on the go. I never knew when he was going to show up at church. Whenever he showed up I knew he was there because there was some type of "silent chaos" going on. He liked to accompany me to other churches. It gave him the opportunity to brush up on his driving skills as he chauffeured me around. He was very diligent about calling me on a very regular basis, even if he did not want anything. The calls were late at night, but he did call.

I think another reason we bonded was because he got a different perspective on how his mother would respond to things he did from me, another adult. Sometimes I would subtly intercede on his behalf with his mother because she knew me from giving him and his sister rides home from church. He would wait around for me after service and we spent a few minutes together riding home on "joke time." So many times, I have had to just shake my head while laughing, and say to him "you are so silly" or "you are so funny."

Things really changed when Charles began to hang out with Iisha and I after church on some Sundays. Sometimes we would go out to eat and other times we would head straight for my house. They knew to leave me alone when I was rushing home to stretch out on my couch. Wherever we were, there were plenty of jokes, funny comments and laughter. That is how I found out he was kind-hearted, thoughtful, helpful, and very, very funny young man. One day he referred to me as "pops." I nearly had a coronary! Me? Old enough to be called, "Pops?" I looked everywhere I could think of in the building for a stick to "beat him down" with. I could not find one so I gratified myself by playfully smacking the back of his round head. He has been calling me "pops" ever since that day.

What I love about these two young men is that they took the initiative to invest their time in getting to know me. They went out of their way to call me and to make personal trips to my house, not even knowing if I was there or not. They are loyal to me and concerned about me, just like all of my other godchildren, my children.

There have been others who have been like children to me that I would like to mention: Dennis and Sabrina in Dallas; Tanya in New Mexico; James Jr. (aka "Player"), EJ, Darien, and DeShaun who are all in the Washington Metropolitan area. I love you and miss you all.

Twenty

Obviously, my two friends, Sean and Herb, who are like my brothers, saw something in my life that I was not giving sufficient attention. For months – No, for years, on different occasions, they both suggested that I write about my life. My initial response was, "yeah, right!"

"What do I have to say about myself that is so important that it needs to be written and published?" After a few more months, and years later, their suggestions became stronger and more frequent. They were becoming more and more emphatic and annoying. My response was still very skeptical.

"Why should I write about my life?"

"Who would want to buy a book about my boring life?

Sean believes that my influence on the lives of youth offers hope to other youth without father figures. And, challenges other males who don't feel capable of being a father figure to give it a shot. Herb believes that people will be amazed by where I came from, in light of where I am today. He calls my life a testimony of what faith in God can do to an individual's life. Within the last few months, their encouraging has become stronger than ever. This time my response was, "OK, I'll do it. Just leave me alone, you're giving me gas!"

The fundamental premise is that the presence of a father figure definitely has a positive influence on the lives of others. Keith, Sean, Herb and I concur that the adult male presence is critical for healthy development of children and youth. Plus, that very same presence stabilizes the households when the father figure is spiritually grounded.

Thus, "Daddy" is also autobiographic because it contains the real life stories of the father figures in my own life and my experience as a father figure to my godchildren and their children. These youth were missing the active presence of an adult male who would fulfill the father role (which all of us have been socialized to expect) and they were longing to be touched and nurtured by the same. They were grappling to have their own need for a father met, and subsequently, cried out to me, "Abba, Father!" I willingly assumed the role, partly because it felt right to say yes when they cried out to me and partly because I unconsciously identified with not having a father figure regularly present in my own experience.

I thank God for the influence of the four very special men who have been father figures to me during specific seasons of my maturation. I am grateful for their willingness to share with me and for the many, many helpful things that they directly and indirectly taught me. I appreciate the fact that my parents sanctioned each of these men as father figures to me. I am grateful that both my parents were unselfish, and wise enough to allow me to have such significant relationships with these gentlemen and their families.

"Daddy" Who me? is a commentary about my own perspective as a father figure who is also a therapist and an ordained Minister of the Gospel by profession. My relationship with my godchildren is a special gift from God. Through them I was able to clearly identify my calling to youth ministry. Also, those relationships gave me direction and shaped my own personal praxis of pastoral theology. In my mind, I was only practicing what I believe in my heart: *everyone deserves to have someone in their corner to love, nurture, and support them regardless how "messed up" their lives may seem to them.* My children have heard that statement many times over and will quickly tell others that I would reach out to anyone in need, particularly a child. What I hope is obvious is my passion for God and the people of God, which is manifested in my life as a

servant in ministry to others. That is what I was taught and that's what I believe.

In writing this book I discovered some things:

1. I noticed the many names that I am called by all of my godchildren.

For clarity, my "*children*" are the adults and my *godchildren* are the younger children. The females call me, "Daddy" or "Father" (jokingly pronounced "Fatha" or "Fava"). The males tend to call me "Dad" or "Pop" or "Pops." The younger generation of godchildren call me "DJ" (So do Monique and Willie). I absolutely love the unique name that the Agee godchildren called me. When "Little DJ" was younger we greeted each other as, "Namesake." Dre couldn't say that so he called me, "amesake." Now, they both call me, "Big DJ."

2. I began to ponder how many of my godchildren actually refer to me as "daddy" in the presence of their biological parents. I was not sure about the males, but the females do. Neither do the new generation godchildren, but they do acknowledge me as their godfather because their parents sanction it and insist that they do so. Even though my adult godchildren see me as a father figure, they recognize that I am not their biological father, but to them that really does not matter. They respect me as "Dad." They acknowledge me by the endearing terms ascribed to paternal fathers and honor me (by words and deeds) like other children do their biological parents.

3. When I said "yes" to these youth and children, I had no idea what I was getting myself into! They had actually chosen

me for the "daddy" role. In retrospect, it meant they had licensed me to be their father figure and agreed to follow me as their family leader in our "new" mutually created surrogate family. Inadvertently, they had also chosen to connect to me, an adult male with other surrogate children and a very large extended family. All of us have reaped benefits from the experience of connecting as a family unit and sharing as an extended family. We have established some very strong bonds of intimacy and a deep sense of gratitude for what we have experienced together. We frequently discuss our experiences of being connected to one another.

The challenge for me was constantly and consciously remembering that each one of my children or godchildren are unique in their own way. They possessed a distinct personality style, temperament, and a diverse mixture of needs, interests, and perspectives. They differed in the manner in which they interacted, communicated, made choices, solved problems, and dealt with conflict. This meant that I had to be sensitive to all the different dynamics as I dealt with each one of them. My approach, discipline, and affirmation was different according to the child I was dealing with at the time. One thing that was consistent was my role with them. My role was to love, guide, and protect them. How I did this was determined by who they were.

They have all heard me say at one time or another, "I love you. When you do good you'll get praise; but when you do bad you'll get jumped!" Accountability and boundaries were definitely something not to be taken lightly. Even though they did not always like or desire to experience the consequences, they knew they could expect both at all times. I must admit, most times I was right on the mark, but there were times I really missed the mark by a mile. But, first I had to admit that I could have done differently. From my confession, our mutual love [kicked in]: They willingly showed me how to father them in ways they could grow from.

4. There are some striking parallels between the Agee and Brower Children. The older children seem to be very much alike in their love for music, while the younger children seem to be alike with regard to their personality and temperament. I have also had the chance to observe the youngest children as they begin to develop their unique personalities. One thing that is different is that I have not had to discipline the Agee children. This observation is not meant to suggest that the Browers do not discipline their children or the Agee children do not need it, but rather to share that my role with the Brower children has included more opportunities for corrective intervention. I appreciate the fact that both sets of parents have encouraged me to use my discretion regarding correcting their children. They have supported me when I have put the "evil eye" on their children and witnessed how quickly their children corrected their behavior because of the look I gave them.

I am honored that their parents chose me to be their godfather to those precious young souls that are in my life. Most times, I feel more like the "grandfather" figure to them because I could easily be a father to their parents based on my age. But regardless to what role I am assigned (or assume) in their impressionable lives, I consider it a privilege to be allowed to love and nurture them. They have added great passion and much joy to my life. They never cease to amaze us by the many creative things they say and do. They really make you laugh. I always look forward to being with them.

5. It takes time to "train up a child" (Proverbs 22:6). It takes perseverance for a parent to discipline (Proverbs. 3:12). It takes effort to teach God's principles (Deuteronomy 4:9) It takes wisdom to be fair (Ephesians 6:4, Colossians 3:21). It takes diligence to manage a family well (1 Timothy 3:12). The truths and principles of the Bible, taught with time, perseverance, effort, wisdom, diligence – that's what we are to give our children. As parents we must have this goal: to teach our children self-control; with firm and loving discipline we'll keep them from the paths of sin. The best gift you can give to your children is your time.

6. Not many men would be willing to accept a surrogate father figure role. It would require them to invest their time, resources and emotion with a child that is not theirs biologically or by marriage. I clearly see traces of each of my father figures in my own character and personality. I can see the fruits of their loving influence. D. Maurice Johnson was created from their cumulative beliefs and attitudes, personality, character and behaviors. My experience has taught me that, just like biological children, godchildren need the love, interest, support, affection, affirmation, advocacy, and nurture of father figures, whether they are biological or surrogate. Let us, male father figures, not miss the opportunities to be a positive influence in the lives of those who desperately need and desire our presence, love, nurture and encouragement.

My surrogate family has been much more interested and interactive in my world than my own biological family, with the exception of Keith, Alice, Kitty, Sundii and Tangy. I do not feel good about the overall lack of interest or interaction from the others. However, I do feel humbled and grateful that so many other people have become my inner circle; treating me like their family and being there for me: Sean, Pattie, Leslie, Donna; and family units like the Agee, Adams, Curtis, Daniels, Hailstock, Henry, Griffin, and Tolliver families. May God's richest blessings also be upon the wonderful people at Metropolitan UMC (Baltimore), Church of the Redeemer UMC (Temple Hills), and Beulah Baptist (DC).

Finally, I am so very grateful for the disciplines of Music, Therapy, Psychology, Theology, and Sociology. Collectively, they have helped to shape my *eclectic* mindset, given me so many priceless experiences and insights, and, the expertise to relate with people from diverse socio-economic and educational backgrounds, in a variety inter-generational, cross-cultural, and ecumenical settings.

If you find this book insightful as an academic, theological, psychological, or therapeutic tool, please feel free to use it for that. My ultimate hope is that you learn more about *being*, or *having* a father figure by simply reading our stories. May God lead you to all the resources needed to bless the lives of others.

EPILOGUE

D. Maurice Johnson

Twenty-One

I have blossomed because of the love, care, comfort and support that I have been shown by my godchildren, their offspring, their parents, and all those who see me and treat me as a father. I am in the process of becoming a foster parent in the state of Maryland so that I can formally help another young boy that I already know blossom in the same way that I have.

Today, "all my children" (no pun intended) are trying to create better lives for themselves. Even though they know Dad loves them and wants what is best for them; they want their dad to be proud of them. And I am! It is comforting to know they love me and are proud of me too.

Monique is doing well in Chicago. She shares a home with her mother and enjoys a career as a professional in the law field. For the past few months we have been dealing with the dynamics of parental issues from the perspective of an adult offspring, and female-male relationship issues. She is having to face some painful realities about the relationships she has experienced within the last few years and regarding the types of men that are attracted to her. She is still very strong-willed and independent, but she is also much more flexible and less critical of herself. She continues to call when she is struggling to be objective, or get other perspectives. She also calls just to talk because she misses me.

Leroy is no longer incarcerated. Praise God, Amen! He and his new wife, Simone reside in Indianapolis. He is working as one of the Directors at the YMCA. He has accepted God's calling into the Gospel Ministry. He has preached his initial sermon and is now a licentiate Baptist Preacher. He has acknowledged and accepted an assignment in youth ministry, which is one of my areas of specialty. You know that I like that! Leroy is trying to re-establish himself in the real world and get adjusted to that, being a preacher, and a married man with a family to take into consideration. I have had the opportunity to meet two of his five children by telephone, and he also has a stepson. It feels strange to hear them call me, "granddad."

Iisha is doing quite well living on her own in a Washington D.C. suburb called, New Carrollton. She is still working as an Editor while simultaneously pursuing a graduate degree in Special Education. She is still struggling to make sense of the male-female relationship battle with a little less drama than in the other ones. She had briefly assumed guardianship for a seventeen-year old girl, named "Nu-Nu." She admits that she now realizes the blessings and curses of parenthood from firsthand experience, so she sees many things differently.

Willie is no longer incarcerated. He is struggling to find work and a steady place of residence. He knew his jail time would cost him something, but I don't think he expected it to last this long or be as frustrating. He also has expanded his family. He already had two sons, now he has a daughter who is nearly a year old. He is grieving the loss of his relationship with his baby's mother and her five-year old son. Willie wants his children to spend more time with granddad as well. Finally, he is learning to accept his consequences and the negative responses without giving up his desire to have a better life. He is realizing that he does not have all the answers and that he must expand his perspective about so many different things. He is facing some really painful realities and not liking what he sees. I feel really bad for him because this struggle is one that he must go through, and overcome, all by himself. All I can do is continue to be a sounding board for him and pray real hard.

Yeolman is away attending Claflin College in South Carolina. He has finally gotten adjusted to being away from home and familiar with the bureaucracy at his school. He speaks of attending graduate school, but I'm not convinced that he is willing to work very hard at achieving that. He is quite ambiguous about the boyfriend-girlfriend thing. Like the rest of us, he is realizing we want a special woman in our life. But some of the antics he has experienced make him very suspicious of their motives and sincerity. There is no perfect mate, but he can try to find a relationship where he feels some semblance of balance between what he expects and what actually exists.

Charles is away attending college in Tennessee. He has a hectic schedule being in the Marching Band, University Choir, Nashville Symphony Chorus, Show Stoppers, a troupe that sings and dances Broadway tunes, and paid vocalist in a church choir. There's no telling how many other irons he has in the fire. He's a night owl so we don't get a chance to talk very much. It is nothing for him to be wide-awake and ready to talk at one or two o'clock in the morning. That's when he and Iisha talk.

Both DJ and Dre, and AJ and Brianna are in school and loving it. DJ and Dre are playing basketball for their school and loving it. AJ and Brianna are cracking the books hard and loving it. They now have a little sister named Taylor. I can't wait to see what type of personality she will have. I am assuming she'll become one of my godchildren even though her parents have not discussed it with me yet. It is just understood that their children will become my godchildren and that's ok with me.

My little ones are growing up so fast it's scary! They are "sprouting up like beanstalks," outgrowing their clothes, sharpening their reasoning skills and powers of deduction. One thing that has remained constant is all of them say and do things that make us roar with laughter. We never know what to expect from them.

As "all my children" are becoming more autonomous, I will not, nor should not be needed in the same ways as before. I have had to let go and respect their individual choices and methods of living their lives. I found them not wanting direction or protection, but rather seeking my sanction of their choices or decisions. They seek my wisdom so that they can exercise good judgment. Instinctively and inevitably this was my ultimate goal, but it sure left me feeling alone. I had gotten accustomed to their worlds being so intertwined in mine, that when the time arrived for them to "roar and soar" I had nothing to fill the void their autonomy created in my life. I wonder if the father figures in my own life experienced similar feelings when I stepped out on my own?

I have extended my family unit to include 3 new daughters: Amanda, Chrissy and Shaunta. Today the family portrait consist of: Monique; Leroy, and his five children - Damien, Jennifer, Jaleesa, Leroy, Desmond, and Devin; Iisha; Willie and his 4 children - Daisean, Melijah, Shirley, and Tracy; Charles; Yeolman; Chrissy; Amanda and her son Jonathan; and Shaunta and her son Jamel. My, how my family has really grown. I love to be with my dozen grandchildren.

My Gallery of Favorite Memories Scrapbook

Monique used to sit on the organ bench with me while I played in church. Every time the preacher got up to preach she would climb in my lap and go to sleep. I don't think she remembers this, but there was not a time that this did not happen. It had become such a frequent routine that members of the church looked at me as they saw me holding her while she slept. If Monique missed church, I would get questions like, "Where is your baby today?" or "I know you missed your baby today." And you know what? They were right about me missing her. Our relationship developed its own set of rituals that even the church anticipated and affirmed.

******

Leroy and I had gone to the mall to buy him a new pair of dress shoes. Every pair of shoes he tried on was too small. I think he must have asked the salesperson to bring him the next half-size larger about three or four different times. When he did finally find a pair that fit they were not his expected size 10, they were a size 11½. He was so shocked and outraged that he decided he did not want ANY new shoes! We turned around and walked out of the store and left the mall completely. Needless to say, he was through shopping for that day. I guess my chuckling at him didn't help either.

******

At about 3:00 a.m. one morning, the phone rang. When I answered it was Iisha's distressed voice pleading, "D-a-a-a-dy? Daddy, Please come down here. I need you to come see me." When? "As soon as you can!" What's happening? "I just need you come down here as soon as possible, please?" Why? (She explained in a REAL short statement, almost in nebulous form.) She was pledging for a sorority and her involvement in the process was really "giving me gas!" I could not stand another late night call listening to her whining. When I did finally arrive two weeks later, I immediately began my search for the sorority leaders who were giving her so much grief. Do you know what she did? She began to plead again! "D-a-a-a-dy? Daddy, Please don't say nothing. I'm gonna really be in big trouble when you

131

leave. They may kick me out and I'm too close to going over. **D-a-a-a-dy**! Daddy, Please don't say nothing, Daddy." I did as she asked, but I did not like it one bit!

******

Willie had been very anxious about the two solos he was about to perform for his high school graduation. One was a Baritone Horn solo and the other was a vocal solo with the gospel choir. Not only was he practicing constantly, but he also expected me to be available to practice with him. WRONG! When graduation day arrived he was a bundle of nerves. His performance on the horn solo had a minor rhythmic flaw, fortunately he was able to recover and complete the song without further incidence. He was so disappointed. Because of the first performance he was really "trippin" hard about the upcoming vocal solo. During the next performance he really surprised us. He lifted his chest high and sang the solo with such ease and accuracy. At the end he used his falsetto range to belt out the final note of the song. Everyone was proud of him, but very shocked because he had worried us to death with his anxiety. Everyone in the house at Constitution Hall was so amazed that they rose to their feet with thunderous cheers and applause.

******

Charles had been itching to "push" my new gray Lexus. I finally gave in on a rainy Sunday afternoon. We were on our way to Iisha's to hang out. I could tell he was a little apprehensive about driving a luxury car, but I kept it to myself. He maintained a good speed, checked his mirror regularly, and signaled properly when switching lanes. He drove well on the beltway (or expressway) and made the appropriate exit. Then, he got a little nervous when he missed the first turn. "Sorry, Pop," he said. "No problem." I directed him to make the very next left turn. He was about to miss that too, when the next thing we heard was the deafening sound of a car horn blasting our ears. Charles was so determined not to miss another turn that he abruptly cut left winding up directly in the path of a speeding car that was headed directly for us! The driver really laid into his horn and swerved into another lane missing us by only a few feet. We were glad he was able to avoid hitting us, but we were a bit shaken from that very close call with danger. Again, he said, "Sorry, Pop. I got a little nervous." I said, "No problem son. That happens to us all at one time or another." When we arrived at Iisha's, she and I had a good chuckle at his expense. I think he was relieved by my calm response but he was still embarrassed – it didn't help that we had laughed at him. Charles begged me not to tell this story but, as you can see, I refused. [Monique's response: "You are so wrong!!!"] **True dat.**

******

I always ask Yeolman who the little "nappy-headed" girls are in his life. Each time I ask him he says there are none. He has concluded that he can't trust any "females" because they always lie to him. Just recently, his mother and I were talking about him and his female friends. She said to me, *"I think Yeolman thinks he's a lover, a lady's man. Let me tell you why. One day I came home and he was in the parking lot talking to this girl. We spoke and I was about to enter the apartment. Then, I decided to be nosey. As I started walking toward them he was beckoning me not to come closer. I went up to the car and said hello to the girl, but I called her by the wrong name. You could have bought Yeolman for a penny! I apologized and went into the apartment. He was furious with me when he came in. He told me that I couldn't be calling names because I don't know who they are. He was right. But why didn't he just say who she was when I walked up to the car? And what was the big deal about mistaking her for someone else? Yeolman didn't fool me! He was concerned that she would find out he was seeing other girls."* We had a good laugh about that encounter. His mother just confirmed what I had already been thinking. There are some girls in his life, probably plenty. **It's all good!** His mother and I both know he is the king of avoidance. He never outright admits to anything unless you press him or he gets busted.

******

It was "little DJ's" fifth birthday. When I arrived at our common meeting place, his grandparent's home, there was a yard sale going on. The whole gang was there: his grandparents, parents, uncles and aunt. I gave him a crisp new five-dollar bill for his present. Then I gave him another dollar because he wanted to buy a soda from the yard sale. He made us all die with laughter a few minutes later. He returned to me and asked, "Hey, where are the rest of my dollar bills? You only gave me one dollar bill, not five!"

******

Dre, his family and I had a movie date. We had some time to spare before for the movie started. We decided to get something to eat at a little shop that was nearby. We had fun - eating and spending time together in fellowship. When everyone had finished eating, I was the only one with a plate still in front of me. Dre said, "Big DJ, are you through eating? I asked him why he wanted to know. In a very stern, almost parental tone, he snapped, "Don't ask me "WHY!" His response was so sincere and emphatic that we just sat there in silence stunned. Us adults turned our heads from his view trying to constraint ourselves from bursting out with laughter. Somehow his mother managed to force herself to respond, "Don't you talk to DJ like that, young man!" Her rebuke was appropriate, but weak. The way Dre had responded to my question was very, very amusing.

AJ" was sitting on the piano bench with me while I was leading the choir in a morning service. He decided he was going to play the piano along with me that day. I repeatedly had to tell him to wait until I told him to play along with me. As the song progressed, I left the piano to conduct the choir acappella (without music). When I had gotten up he was playing the Congo alongside his father who was on the drums. During a silent break in between the phrases, "AJ" made us all laugh because he began hitting the keys hard enough that the sound was quite apparent. You could hear the audience laughing with surprise. After the song, the pastor teasingly told the church, "Dr. Johnson, had better do his job or AJ will be our new musician."

******

Brianna, her father and I were sitting in church together. She climbed into my lap with her book bag and bag of goodies. She got settled comfortably and began searching through the book bag. After a few minutes she pulled out a book about Barbie. She began showing me pictures and interpreting them for me. Then, she showed me that Barbie was wearing stick-on clothes. In one picture the clothing was not aligned properly. I said, "Look, Brianna, her clothes are not very well. You can see her underwear." Brianna replied, "Yeah and her boobs." Her father and chuckled silently trying to ignore her observations so she repeated it. "You can see her boobs." This time she laughed. We tried very hard to ignore her the second time.

******

Christmas this year showed me how energized I get by playing with "pop-pop's" babies: Shirley and Tracy, Jonathan and Jamel. I am proud to be their surrogate grandfather.

******

Being a father figure seems to be a never-ending cycle. It seems as if children have built-in radar detectors that spot you and makes them gravitate toward you. You try to resist them but can't, because they will cling to you even tighter. Even when successful in resisting the urge to father, there is always another needy child out there lurking in shadows, waiting for their opportunity to be showered with love and care. I have come to accept this gift as my calling in life and my way to make a meaningful contribution to this world: by touching one life at a time. I believe **every person is special and needs someone in their corner that makes them feel special and wanted.**

Whether you are a parent or father figure, you don't have to always be right or have all the answers. But, you do need to **be consistently present, patient, understanding, sensitive, honest, accountable and flexible**. To be challenged by your child allows them a safe place to learn the skills for effective communication, conflict resolve and problem solving. They will not just wake up one day equipped with those skills. Show them and let them practice on you regularly!

One last thing, **touch [affection] is extremely important to your child**. Hugs, kisses on the forehead or jaw, playfully twinkling ears and noses, pats on the head, rubbing or patting the shoulders or arms, love taps, or even wrestling - if you are still able – allows them to feel connected with you. Every one of my children and grandchildren know that I will kiss their face and hug them at anytime. And it may happen all in one swift movement! If I have been missing them and really glad to see them, I may hug them, kiss both sides of their face and them hug them again. I repeat, all in one swift movement. From your touch, your children will also learn to discern when you are being serious or being playful and the difference between safe touch and inappropriate touch. Know this: You need touches from your children, too! **A touch from your child can be soothing to you** as well.

Now, to all the teens out there without a dad regularly present all the time - I believe I know how you feel. Life may not be easy for you, but **you can find all the help you need in God.** Believe me, **"God can, and will, be a father to you!"** He is the Father of all fathers. If you ask, He may send a man who is willing to be a father to you. You may not even know the man! That's what he did for me and I don't ever remember asking him for one. In my short lifetime, God has sent SEVERAL father figures to me. Then, he turned around and used me to be a father figure to several children (who were teens at the time) AND a Godfather to several young children. Each time I hear one of my children say kind things about me as their dad, I am grateful that God has done a great thing in their life and greatly humbled that I have had the privilege of being included in their journey. In light of all this, I willingly say, "Bring on the new ones; Let the journey continue! To God be the glory!

[Hush, Keith.]

D. Maurice Johnson

When you know that you're with people who want to help and share,
When you know that they really love you and like to have you there,
When you know that you can be yourself and just relax a while,
When you know that you can always find a cheery word or smile,
When you know that come what may you are not facing it alone,
Then you know you're with family...you know that you are at home.

Rita Heyden

ABOUT THE BOOK

"Daddy" Who Me? Is an autobiographic narrative, a mosaic about my relationship to my own father, the contributions of other father figures in my life, personal reflections about my godchildren and their perspective of me as a godfather.

—D. Maurice Johnson
Washington, DC, 2001

ABOUT THE AUTHOR

Dr. D. Maurice Johnson (aka "DJ") is a native of East Chicago, Indiana. He is a Professional Ministry Consultant who specializes in Gospel Music Ministry. He has a deep passion for music ministry to God's people, especially to youth. His entire life has been about music ministry that points others to Christ. He is *CEO and Founder* of Majestic Ones, a professional Ministry Consulting firm, a *Lecturer*, and an *Instructor of Gospel Music*. He currently serves as *Minister of Music & Arts* for Metropolitan United Methodist Church in Baltimore, Maryland. He is a *Registered Music Therapist* for Wickersty and Associates in Cheverly, Maryland. He provides therapeutic creative arts services to children and adolescents with emotional, behavioral and learning challenges. Dr. Johnson also serves as a *Faculty Instructor* in the Academic Division of the Gospel Music Workshop of America and Head of the Applied Music Division in the Artelia Hutchins Institute of the National Convention of Gospel Choruses and Choirs. His publications are entitled: *Skilled Excellence*, *These Are They*, *Gospelized Hymns*, *Gospelized Communion Hymns*, *Just for the King*, and *Fit for the King*.

"I'm just trying to tell everybody, about SOMEBODY who can save anybody.
God is somebody you need to know!"

PEN